Goodwill and Its Treatment in Accounts

Also from Westphalia Press

westphaliapress.org

The Idea of the Digital University

Dialogue in the Roman-Greco World

The History of Photography

International or Local Ownership?: Security Sector Development in Post-Independent Kosovo

Lankes, His Woodcut Bookplates

Opportunity and Horatio Alger

The Role of Theory in Policy Analysis

Natural Gas as an Instrument of Russian State Power

Non Profit Organizations and Disaster

The Idea of Neoliberalism: The Emperor Has Threadbare Contemporary Clothes

Social Satire and the Modern Novel

Ukraine vs. Russia: Revolution, Democracy and War: Selected Articles and Blogs, 2010-2016

James Martineau and Rebuilding Theology

A Strategy for Implementing the Reconciliation Process

Issues in Maritime Cyber Security

Growing Inequality: Bridging Complex Systems, Population Health and Health Disparities

Designing, Adapting, Strategizing in Online Education

Gunboat and Gun-runner

Pacific Hurtgen: The American Army in Northern Luzon, 1945

New Frontiers in Criminology

Understanding Art

Homeopathy

Fishing the Florida Keys

Iran: Who Is Really In Charge?

Contracting, Logistics, Reverse Logistics: The Project, Program and Portfolio Approach

The Thomas Starr King Dispute

Springfield: The Novel

Alchemy: Ancient and Modern

Lariats and Lassos

Mr. Garfield of Ohio

The French Foreign Legion

War in Syria

Naturism Comes to the United States

Feeding the Global South

The History of Men's Raiment

Goodwill and Its Treatment in Accounts

A Historical Look at Goodwill, Trade Marks & Trade Names

---

by Lawrence R. Dicksee and Frank Tillyard

WESTPHALIA PRESS
An imprint of Policy Studies Organization

Westphalia Press
An imprint of Policy Studies Organization
1527 New Hampshire Ave., NW
Washington, D.C. 20036
info@ipsonet.org

ISBN-13: 978-1-63391-613-5
ISBN-10: 1-63391-613-8

Cover design by Jeffrey Barnes:
jbarnesbook.design

Daniel Gutierrez-Sandoval, Executive Director
PSO and Westphalia Press

Updated material and comments on this edition
can be found at the Westphalia Press website:
www.westphaliapress.org

GOODWILL

AND

ITS TREATMENT IN ACCOUNTS

BY

LAWRENCE R. DICKSEE, M.Com., F.C.A.

*Professor of Accounting and Business Organisation in the
University of London,*

AND

FRANK TILLYARD, M.A. (Oxon.), M.Com.

BARRISTER-AT-LAW,

Professor of Commercial Law at the University of Birmingham.

FOURTH EDITION.

LONDON :

GEE & CO. (PUBLISHERS) LTD., 14 QUEEN VICTORIA STREET, E.C.4.

1920.

BY THE SAME AUTHOR.

PRICE

"ADVANCED ACCOUNTING." (Fifth Edition) - - 22/6

"AUDITING." (Eleventh Edition) - - - 16/-

"BOOKKEEPING FOR ACCOUNTANT STUDENTS." (Seventh Edition) - - - - - - 6/-

"BOOKKEEPING FOR COMPANY SECRETARIES." (Fifth Edition) - - - - - - 6/-

"BOOKKEEPING EXERCISES FOR ACCOUNTANT STUDENTS." (Third Edition) - - - 4/-

"AUCTIONEERS' ACCOUNTS." (Third Edition) - - 4/-

"SOLICITORS' ACCOUNTS." (Second Edition) - - 4/-

"DEPRECIATION, RESERVES, AND RESERVE FUNDS." (Third Edition) - - - - - 4/-

"HOTEL ACCOUNTS." (Second Edition) - - - 4/-

"MINES ACCOUNTING AND MANAGEMENT." - - 6/-

"OFFICE MACHINERY AND APPLIANCES." (Second Edition) - - - - - - 10/6

(*Published by Gee & Co. (Publishers) Ltd., 14 Queen Victoria Street, London, E.C. 4.*)

"OFFICE ORGANISATION AND MANAGEMENT" (with H. E. Blain). (Fourth Edition) - - - 7/6

(*Published by Sir Isaac Pitman & Sons, Ltd., 1 Amen Corner, Paternoster Row, E.C. 4.*)

"THE A B C OF BOOKKEEPING." - - - 2/6

"BUSINESS ORGANISATION." (Second Edition) - - 5/-

(*Published by Longman's, Green & Co., 29 Paternoster Row, E.C. 4.*)

"BUSINESS METHODS AND THE WAR." - - - 2/-

(*Published by The Cambridge University Press, Fetter Lane, E.C. 4.*)

CONTENTS.

		PAGE
PREFACE TO THIRD EDITION		v
PREFACE TO FOURTH EDITION	.. ..	viii
CHAPTER I.—The Connection between Goodwill and Trade Names and Trade Marks	..	1
II.—The Nature of Trade Names and their Protection	.. .. ..	10
III.—Trade Marks and their Protection	..	21
IV.—The Nature of Goodwill	.. ..	43
V.—The Assignment of Goodwill		52
VI.—Partnership and Goodwill	..	64
VII.—Goodwill and Accounts		70
VIII.—The Valuation of Goodwill	..	74
IX.—The Fluctuations of Goodwill		88
X.—The Purchase of Goodwill	..	97
XI.—Goodwill in Partnership Accounts	..	107
XII.—Goodwill in Companies' Accounts	..	131
APPENDIX A.—Text of the Trade Marks Act 1905 and 1919	.. ..	143
B.—Common Form Clauses relating to Goodwill	.. ..	173
INDEX TO CASES	..	176
GENERAL INDEX		180

PREFACE TO THIRD EDITION.

THE First Edition of this work, which was published in 1897, was founded upon a lecture delivered by the author at a meeting of the Birmingham Chartered Accountant Students' Society in the autumn of the previous year. Numerous *pro formâ* examples were, however, appended to still further explain the principles laid down in the body of the work, and a valuable "introductory chapter" on the law relating to Goodwill was supplied by the late Mr. T. M. Stevens, D.C.L., Barrister-at-Law.

The Second Edition, which was issued in 1900, was but little more than a reprint of the first, save that the leading decisions which had been given between 1897 and 1900 were duly noted. It is, however, of interest to note that in the meantime the idea which was, I believe, first enunciated in this work—namely, that interest on capital and the value of a proprietor's time while engaged in the management of a business were both factors to be taken into account before arriving at the marketable value of Goodwill—began to find acceptance, and had been specially referred to in a lecture delivered by the late Mr. Edwin Guthrie, F.C.A., at a meeting of the Chartered Accountant Students' Society of London in 1898. Even then, however, the principle that the Goodwill of a business acquired by a joint-stock company should be paid for out of premiums derived from the issue of its share capital had by no means been generally recognised and, so far as the author has been able to ascertain, "Answers," Lim., was the only new company whose shares had been issued at a premium in order to enable this question of Goodwill to be dealt with upon a scientific basis.

During the last few years events have occurred which can hardly have failed to bring home to the minds of the thoughtful student the inherent soundness of the principles laid down by the author nearly ten years since. Whatever other causes may have been at work, it will probably now be very generally admitted that the effect of further issues of capital by an established company, either at par or at a premium less than the price commanded in the market by the existing shares, is to "water" the capital of the undertaking as a whole—and therefore to cause a fall in the market value of its shares. Without going into particulars, and without seeking to cast any reflection upon existing undertakings, it is thought that it must at the present time be admitted that the fall that has taken place in the shares of the British South Africa Co., of the Aerated Bread Company, Lim., and of most British Railways (all of which for a number of years past have been systematically issuing new capital *pro ratá* to their existing shareholders at a price lower than the current market rate) has directly contributed towards reducing the market values of these several securities. A principle that holds good with regard to an established undertaking must, of course, be equally sound when applied to a new company taking over an established business ; and for these reasons I see no ground for modifying the views which I expressed in the first edition of this work. At that time there was, it is true, a practical objection to the singling out of the item "Goodwill" for such special treatment, in that it drew prominent attention to the amount that it was proposed to pay for this somewhat elusive asset ; but inasmuch as the provisions of the Companies Act, 1900*, now require the price to be paid for the "Goodwill" to be separately stated in every prospectus,

---

* Now incorporated in Section 81, Sub-section 1 (g), of the Companies (Consolidation) Act, 1908.

there can be no possible reason for persistence in old and unscientific methods, inasmuch as they have been at last (and very properly) shorn of all practical advantages.

In the present edition the legal introduction, which is comprised in the first seven chapters, has been entirely re-written by my colleague, Mr. Frank Tillyard, and greatly amplified. Indeed this portion of the subject has been so fully dealt with that I venture to think that the work is now entitled to take its place as a legal text-book. It should be added, however, that it has been written, not from the point of view of lawyers and law students, but of practical business men, and that nothing has been taken for granted with which it would be unreasonable to assume that they were acquainted. The remaining five chapters, enunciating general business principles and explaining their practical application, are elucidated with the aid of numerous *pro formâ* examples which, it is hoped, will be found intelligible even to those who are not skilled accountants. The full text of the Trade Marks Act, 1905, is appended, as that useful measure would appear to be far less known to business men than its importance renders desirable; while the second appendix, dealing with the more customary forms of clauses in deeds of partnership, &c., relating to the treatment of Goodwill, will, it is thought, be found suggestive, no less on account of what it may be found expedient to avoid in them, than by reason of the merits which they undoubtedly possess. The Index to Cases will be found of considerable value to students, and others, desirous of readily ascertaining the exact practical effect of such decisions as have been given from time to time; while the General Index, which concludes the volume, will doubtless render it more serviceable as a book of reference, both to the practising accountant and to the man of business.

LAWRENCE R. DICKSEE.

48 Copthall Avenue,
7th June 1906.

PREFACE TO FOURTH EDITION.

THE fourth edition of "Goodwill and its Treatment in Accounts" has been long overdue, but the pre-occupations of war work have prevented me from devoting the necessary time to its preparation until quite recently. The somewhat numerous enquiries that I have received from all quarters while the book was out of print serve to show, however, that it supplies a need that is somewhat acutely felt in the business world.

The first portion of the new edition, dealing with the legal aspect of the matter, has been very carefully revised and brought up to date by my colleague, Professor Tillyard. The latter portion, for which I personally am responsible, has also been carefully revised and in parts re-written, and I have taken advantage of the present opportunity to say something upon the subject of advertising in connection with Goodwill, and also concerning "watered" Capital and issues of bonus shares. While making no claim to completeness, I venture to hope that this volume will be found of value not merely to the accountant student, but also to the practitioner and to business men generally.

LAWRENCE R. DICKSEE.

Lincoln House,
　296-302, High Holborn, W.C. 1.
　　19th June 1920.

Goodwill and its Treatment in Accounts.

CHAPTER I.

THE CONNECTION BETWEEN GOODWILL AND TRADE NAMES AND TRADE MARKS.

BEFORE we come to a study of the law of our subject let us for a moment look at it as it presents itself to our minds in everyday business life. We see, for instance, in the business world a man—A.—starting a fresh business (for our present purpose let us say the manufacture of some article), either under his own name or under some name assumed for trade reasons. He works hard, pushes his business judiciously, advertises largely, and after some years his name becomes a household word, and the articles he manufactures are very widely known. We feel at once that beyond his works, his machinery, and his stock-in-trade, A. has something else, much more intangible, but none the less valuable, which for the moment we may describe as the reputation of his name and goods, or more succinctly as "his business," using that term as it is familiarly used as denoting something more than the material assets. We examine A.'s books, but we find no entry to correspond with this intangible property. But we may be certain that A. attaches value to it, for the moment it is attacked he invokes the aid of the Courts of Law, and protects his property by the most powerful of all remedies—viz., that known technically as an injunction. For instance, B., a competitor, uses a name resembling A.'s trade name in such a way as to take away business from A. ; or by the use of trade-marks resembling A.'s trade-marks, B., his competitor, passes off his goods as A.'s goods. When this occurs A. promptly asks for an injunction to restrain his competitor B. from so invading his rights.

So long as the original business is carried on by the original creator of it this intangible property only comes to the surface when it is necessary to take some steps for its protection, and we shall find our law under the headings "Trade Names" and "Trade Marks," and the key-note of these cases is the word "protection." Now we may take this a step further. There will come a time when our business man himself, or his executors after his death, will want to sell his business, and he or they will want to realise this intangible property along with the works, stock-in-trade, and other visible and tangible assets. What he can pass on to another of this intangible property is commonly known as "Goodwill." We need not concern ourselves at present with elaborate definitions of this term. Let us take the summary given by Mr. Justice Warrington in a recent case (*Hill v. Fearis*, 1905, 1 Ch. 466) :—"The Goodwill of a "business is the advantage, whatever it may be, which a person "gets by continuing to carry on and being entitled to repre- "sent to the outside world that he is carrying on a business "which has been carried on for some time previously. That "seems to me to be the meaning of Goodwill." Or we may take what Lord Justice Lindley said in *The Commissioners of Inland Revenue v. Muller, Lim.* (1901, A.C. 217) :—"Good- "will regarded as property has no meaning except in connec- "tion with some trade, business, or calling. In that connec- "tion I understand the word to include whatever adds value "to a business by reason of situation, name and reputation, "connection, introduction to old customers, and agreed absence

" from competition, or any of these things, and there may be
" others which do not occur to me."

As we are now looking at this intangible property from the
point of view of its realisation and transfer, there are naturally
fresh incidents of it which become material. As counsel for the
plaintiff in the case of *Hill v. Fearis*, just quoted, said in his
argument, " Goodwill involves a right to represent that you are
" carrying on the business of the firm, to solicit the customers
" of the old firm, to have the books of the firm, and to prevent
" anybody else from saying that he is carrying on the business.
" That is quite apart from the right to use the name of the firm."
In other words, when a man is merely protecting his own business no question can arise as to soliciting customers, or the right
to books, but when he is transferring (as far as it can be done)
his business, then questions of books, and lists of customers, and
the solicitation of customers, become relevant and material.
These questions may become even more complicated when the
Goodwill is the property of two or more persons in partnership.
But we want to lay complications aside, and get into our minds
this primary conception of a " business," which is more than
the tangible assets which are attached to it. The commercial
phrase, " to be sold as a going concern," will help us. The
difference between the works sold separately, the stock-in-trade
sold separately, and so on, and " the business " sold as a whole
—works, stock-in-trade, Goodwill, and all—is the difference
between a horse alive and working and the same horse as hide
and cats' meat.

This idea of " the business," and the Goodwill of a business,
as distinct from its tangible assets, is fundamental in English
law on the subject, and this is abundantly clear when we are
dealing with the realisation and transfer of Goodwill, Trade
Names, and Trade Marks. Trade names and trade marks are
component parts of " the business," and can be separately

protected, if separately endangered, but cannot be transferred apart from "the business." In technical language, English law holds both the assignment of a trade name in gross and the assignment of a trade mark in gross to be void. (The meaning of the term "in gross" can be illustrated from the law of common rights. If the owner of a particular cottage in a village has the right to turn cattle on to the common, and this right passes with the ownership of the cottage, then the owner has a right of common appendant. A person who has a right of common irrespective of the ownership of any property has a right of common in gross.) And the converse holds good—namely, that a transfer of "a business," or the "goodwill of a business," carries without further words the right to use the trade name and the trade marks used in and attached to the business transferred. It will be worth our while to consider here an authority for each of these propositions.

The question of the validity of an isolated assignment of a trade name arose in the case of *Thorniloe v. Hill* (1894, 1 Ch. 569). The facts in that case were as follows:—John Forrest was a well-known London watchmaker, and watches bearing his name were well-known in the watchmaking trade. Carley & Co. bought the Goodwill of John Forrest's business, and afterwards made an assignment of their property in favour of their creditors. The trustee under this assignment sold Carley & Co.'s "business" to one purchaser, and then made a separate sale and assignment of "the name, title, and goodwill of John Forrest, London," to Thorniloe. Hill was a rival watchmaker, who, without any title at all, put John Forrest, London, on the watches he made. Thorniloe sought to restrain Hill by injunction from using the name John Forrest, London, on the ground that he had bought the exclusive right to use that name. The Court held that even if anything was assigned to Thorniloe by the trustee of Carley & Co. it was merely the right to use the name John Forrest, London, *unconnected with any business*, and, being a mere assignment in gross, was invalid. The reason for this connection between the assignment of the trade name and the assignment of " the business," or " the Goodwill of the business," was given as follows in that case by Romer, L.J. (then Mr. Justice Romer) : " Now, speaking " generally, a purchaser of a business, if he continues it, has the " right to use the trade name and trade marks of the business· " in any way he pleases which is not calculated to deceive. And, " in particular, as a rule the purchaser of a business may mark " goods made by him *in the course of that business* with the name " of the vendor, although the vendor, or his old workmen, did " not make or assist in making such goods, and by so marking " the goods the purchaser would not be considered as doing that " which was calculated to deceive his customers or the public. " The reason of that is that in most cases, especially where the " purchaser is continuing the business, the mark in the vendor's " name might fairly be held to be only a representation that the " goods were manufactured in the course of the business, without " any representation as to the persons by whom that business " was being carried on, and there would be no substantial risk " of deception." And he then goes on to discuss special cases where there would be a risk of deception. The assignment of a trade name in gross and apart from any business is bound to lead to deception, and is therefore not allowed by English law.

The question of the validity of an isolated assignment of a trade mark arose in the case of *Pinto v. Badman* (1891, 8 R.P.C. 181). The value of this case from the point of principle is that it covers the case of an unregistered trade mark. Section 70 of the Patent Act of 1883 had expressly enacted that " a trade " mark, when registered, shall be assigned and transmitted only " in connection with the Goodwill of the business concerned in " the particular goods, or classes of goods, for which it has been " registered, and shall be determinable with that Goodwill." (See now Section 22 of the Trade Marks Act, 1905, *post* p. 139.)

The plaintiff in this case claimed the exclusive right to brand cigars with a certain trade name or mark. When he took an assignment of it it was an unregistered trade mark, but he subsequently registered it, and the material facts as to his acquisition of the trade mark appear from the following passage in Lord Esher's judgment :—" Now the origin is shown of the " plaintiff's right to use this registration. The manufacturers in " Mexico, of the name of Garcia, were the people who had the " original right. How had they got that right ? They had pro- " cured that right by manufacturing cigars of a peculiar kind, by " importing those cigars into England, and obtaining by reason " of their manufacture and skill a considerable character or value " for those cigars ; and they had by using a label with regard to " those cigars which they had thus sold procured a right to the " exclusive use in England of that label as applied to their " cigars. The label had become valuable. Why ? It had " become a valuable label to them because it intimated to the " purchasers of cigars in England that the cigars sold with that " label were of the valued—I do not say valuable—but the " esteemed and valued manufacture of Garcia & Co. They had " that right. What did they sell to Rendon ? Inasmuch as " Rendon took Pinto into partnership, what did they sell to " Rendon ? In my opinion .   .   .   .   all they sold was their " right which they had to use the label or trade mark which they " had used. Therefore they sold to Rendon and Pinto, the " plaintiffs, the right to use the trade mark which had become " known and appreciated in England as an indication that the " cigars sold with it were sold from Garcia's, and from their " manufactory. *Therefore all they sold was the trade mark.* " They sold no part of their business of which the trade mark " was an indication. They retained and kept the right to carry " on their business just precisely as they had before, and even to " import into England the very same cigars they had always " imported. .   Inasmuch as there was nothing sold but

" the right to the trade mark, I come to the conclusion that the
" law of England does not allow the purchaser of such a right,
" when he purchases the right only, to register that trade mark,
" the right to register which, as between himself and the seller,
" has passed to him." Lord Justice Fry said :—" It is plain
" the question comes to be one of law, and by English law can a
" trader, who has used a brand upon a particular article, and
" who continues to manufacture that article, alienate that brand
" to another person, so as to give that alienee any right what-
" ever? It appears to me that upon first principles he can have
" no such right. The brand is an indication of origin, and if
" you transfer the indication of origin, without transferring the
" origin itself, you are transferring a right, if any right at all,
" to commit a fraud upon the public, and such right is not recog-
" nised by the law of England. . . . Before and after
" registration a trade mark cannot be assigned independently of
" the manufacture of the goods to which it relates."

The converse case that an assignment of the Goodwill carries
the trade marks was decided in *Shipwright v. Clements* (1871,
19 W.R. 599), in which an outgoing partner sold his interest to
his late partner. Part of the partnership property was a perfume
known as Zingari Bouquet. The outgoing partner claimed the
right to go on selling this perfume under that name. But it was
held that if a business were sold without any word being said
about the trade mark, the mark would be understood and held
to pass to the purchaser.

To sum up these introductory remarks, we may say that
English commerce and English law agree in recognising in an
old established business, with its distinctive name, and with or
without trade marks, an intangible asset, which, within certain
limits imposed to prevent public deception, is freely transfer-
able under the well-known term of Goodwill. The enjoyment of
this asset will be protected by the law, either as a whole, or in
other circumstances only as regards the trade name or trade

mark which may be endangered.   But the law does not recognise
a trade name, or a trade mark, as an assignable right or asset
apart from the Goodwill of the business in connection with
which the trade name, or trade mark, has been used; and the
ground of this refusal is the danger of fraud upon the public.

Goodwill, when once created, may be kept alive with its
attendant trade names and trade marks for generations, but it
is not necessarily immortal, and it follows from the cases already
examined that if the Goodwill of a business perishes, the trade
names and trade marks will perish also.   In the case of *In re
Registered Trade Mark of Sidney Ord & Co.* (1913, 30 R.P.C.
725) the process of the decay of a Goodwill may be seen, and
the time of its ultimate dissolution is pointed out.   In this
case the plaintiff, whose name was not Sidney Ord, built up
a business as a manufacturer of jam and marmalade, and in
February, 1894, he registered a trade mark consisting of the
supposed signature of Sidney Ord.   In 1908 the plaintiff
became mentally infirm, and was still in that condition when
the action was started.   The business was carried on for a year
or two by a receiver, but without success, and in December 1909
the business, together with the Goodwill, plant, and the lease
of the premises on which it was carried on, was put up for
sale, but was not sold.   In April 1910 the premises were let
on lease for another purpose, and the plant, stock-in-trade, pots,
jars, &c. were sold separately.   The book debts were realised
and the account books burnt.   The Goodwill and the trade
mark were not disposed of.   The plaintiff's manager took
service with another firm who began to sell marmalade bearing
labels in which the name " Sidney Ord " was prominent.   The
plaintiff brought an action against this firm for an infringement of his trade mark, and they, in their turn, moved to
expunge the trade mark from the register.

It was held that the Goodwill of the plaintiff's business came
to an end when the premises were, so to speak, gutted and handed

over for the purpose of another business, and when the original business was in fact abandoned. As the trade mark could only exist by virtue of its attachment to the Goodwill, it perished with the Goodwill.

It was also held that the trade mark not being attached to the goods in respect of which it was registered, and having no Goodwill to support it, was a danger to the trading community which the applicants, or any trader desiring to adopt the name it contained in his trade, were, as aggrieved persons, entitled to have removed from the register under Sections 22 and 35 of the Trade Marks Act 1905.

We shall now proceed to discuss more in detail the legal incidents of Trade Names, Trade Marks, and Goodwill. We shall finally see to what extent, if any. the law has anything to say as to the treatment in accounts of this intangible asset, or whether it leaves the problem entirely to accountants.

CHAPTER II.

THE NATURE OF TRADE NAMES AND THEIR PROTECTION.

IT is sometimes said that a man has a right to trade under any name he may choose. This is just as true and just as untrue as to say that a man may in England say anything he pleases. We have the right of free speech and liberty of the Press in England, but still a man must not say things to the injury of other people. There are no arbitrary limits to our liberty of speech, but there is a law of libel. In the same way, a man's general right to trade under any name he may choose is not subject to any arbitrary limitations, but is subject to objection at the instance of other persons who may be injured by the use of the particular name he has adopted. Quite recently *registration* of business names has been made obligatory by the Registration of Business Names Act, 1916. The same rule applies in general to companies registered under the Companies Act, 1862, subject to certain statutory provisions as to the registration of names, and the use of the registered name. For instance, it has been enacted that the Registrar of Joint Stock Companies shall not register a company with a name identical with that by which a subsisting company is already registered, or so nearly resembling the same, as to be calculated to deceive. But the decision of the Registrar to register company A with a particular name is no bar to an action by company B, already registered, to restrain company A from carrying on business under a name which company B alleges is doing it an injury. The general law on the subject was laid down with admirable clearness by Sir George Jessel in the case of the *Merchant Banking Co. of London, Lim. v. Merchants' Joint Stock Bank* (1878, 9 Ch.D. 563), which was an action brought by the former company to restrain the latter company from carrying on its business under a name so similar to its own.   In the course of his judgment the Master of the Rolls said :—" As the law originally stood I think " that any person might use his own name for the purpose of " trade, and might use any fancy name for the purpose of trade. " If a man's name was Brown or Jones he was not compelled, " according to the common law. to carry on trade under the name " of Brown or Jones, but might carry on trade under any fancy " name he chose, and the mere fact of somebody else having the " same name and carrying on trade under that name does not " prevent another person from doing the same. If John Brown " sells coals another John Brown may sell potatoes, and there " is no law that I know of to prevent him from selling his pota- " toes under the name of John Brown. The first John Brown " could not in such a case restrain the second John Brown from " carrying on trade under his own name. Again, nothing can be " plainer than that if the first John Brown carried on business " under the name not of John Brown, but of John Brown & Co., " so might the second. What the law did prevent was fraud ; " and it prevented not only actual fraud—that is, fraud inten- " tionally committed—but it also prevented a man from carry- " ing on business in such a way, whether he knew it or not, as " to represent that his business was the business of another man. " And it might happen that the mere using a well-known fancy " name would be evidence of an intention on the part of a " person using it to commit a fraud.   One can well understand " a certain fancy name being so attached to a business as to " indicate that business. and that business alone, and that " another man using the same fancy name in carrying on a " similar business ought to be convicted of an intention to

" defraud from that circumstance alone.   That might well be;
" but still, after all, it is merely a question of evidence.   Now
" we have had the question before the Courts of Equity over
" and over again.   There is the well-known case of *Croft v. Day*
" (1843, 7 Beav. 84)—the case of Day & Martin, the blacking
" makers in Holborn—in which there was no longer either a Day
" or a Martin, as in the original firm, both being long since dead,
" and the persons before the Court, who then carried on their
" business, deriving title under them, were held entitled to
" restrain a real ' Day ' and a real ' Martin ' from trading under
" the name of Day & Martin as makers of blacking, because it
" was a manufacture of the well-known firm of ' Day & Martin,'
" the reason for the injunction being that the name of Day &
" Martin had been adopted for the purpose of representing and
" holding out to the public that it was the old firm of Day &
" Martin.   There   is   another   well-known   case,   I   believe
" unreported, that of Mr. Newman, the colourman, of Soho
" Square.   It was held that he was entitled to restrain another
" Newman, who bore the name of Newman, from setting up a
" shop as colourman a few doors off, and advertising himself as
" Newman & Co.   There the Court held that there was an
" intention to appropriate the first Newman's business under the
" pretence of *bonâ fide* trading under that name."   He then goes
on to consider whether registration under the Companies Act,
1862, makes any difference, and decides "that really the right
after registration is exactly the same right as before."

In another case, which also dealt with the larger question of
Goodwill, *Levy v. Walker* (1879, 10 Ch.D. 436), James, L.J.,
laid down the following general principle (p. 447) :—" A man
" has the right to say, ' You must not use a name, whether ficti-
" ' tious or real; you must not use a description, whether true
" ' or not, which is intended to represent, or calculated to repre-
" ' sent to the world that your business is my business, and so by
" ' a fraudulent misstatement deprive me of the profits of the

" ' business which would otherwise have come to me.' That is
" the principle, and the sole principle, on which this Court
" interferes. The Court interferes solely for the purpose of
" protecting the owner of a trade or business from a fraudulent
" invasion of that business by somebody else. It does not inter-
" fere to prevent the world outside from being misled into
" anything. If there is any misleading, that may be for the
" Criminal Courts of the country to take notice of, or for the
" Attorney-General to interfere with ; but an individual plaintiff
" can only proceed on the ground that, having established a
" business reputation under a particular name, he has a right to
" restrain anyone else from injuring his business by using that
" name."

In a quite recent case in the Court of Appeal the question was
definitely raised as to the right of the Court to put an absolute
veto on the use of a man's real name, even for the protection of
an existing business with the same name. This was in the case
of *Cash v. Cash* (1902, 19 R.P.C. 181), in which the plaintiffs
were J. & J. Cash, Lim., of Coventry, the proprietors of Cash's
frillings, Cash's woven names, &c., and the defendant was
Joseph Cash, who also manufactured and sold frillings at
Coventry, and who traded as Joseph Cash & Co. Vaughan
Williams, L.J., said :—" It may be that a trade is of such a
" nature that the products of the trade will become almost indis-
" solubly connected with the business carried on by a particular
" manufacturer, who, it may be, created the particular trade ;
" but still, even though that may be so, and even though such
" fact is to be taken into consideration in an action for an
" injunction, there never has been a case yet in which an order
" has been made restraining a man altogether from carrying on
" in his own name a particular trade. Every decision that has
" as yet been given has been limited to restraining him from
" carrying on such trade, so identified with the plaintiff's busi-
" ness, without taking the steps which an honest man ought to

" wish to take to prevent his goods being confounded with the
" plaintiff's goods, whose goods are so much identified with the
" particular trade."

Vaughan Williams, L.J., put it pithily in this wise :—" An
" honest man will wish to take all reasonable precautions to
" prevent his goods being confounded with the goods of other
" traders.   If a man is not an honest man, then the law will step
" in, and compel him to behave like one."

We shall see in the next section that a trade mark is recognised as " property."   This is not true of a trade name.   This
was pointed out by Lindley, L.J., in the case of *Powell v. The
Birmingham Vinegar Co.* (1896, 2 Ch. 64) as follows :—
" Limits have been put to the 'right to complain of the use of
" words which have not been put to the right to complain of the
" use of marks. For example, if a man uses his own name to denote
" his own goods it would be intolerable to confer upon him the
" right to prevent other people of the same name from honestly
" using their own name to denote their own goods, even although
" they might be of the same kind as his and be indistinguishable
" from them.   .   .   Yet even in such a case, if the descriptive
" name is proved to mean the goods of the plaintiff, and *if
" deception is also proved*, a person may be restrained from
" using such name or word without taking such steps as will
" render mistakes unlikely to occur."

In the case of *Jamieson v. Jamieson* (1898, 15 R.P.C. 169)
Vaughan Williams, L.J., amplified this (p. 191) :—" You cannot
" habitually use inaccurate words in relation to matters of law
" without running a risk of arriving at propositions which are
" not true in law.   One of the most striking illustrations of that
" is that throughout the argument counsel used observations
" based upon an assumption that a trader whose goods had come
" to be known either under a particular trade name, or had come
" to be known as being denoted by the trader's own name,

"acquired thereby some sort of right of property in that trade "name, or in the use of that name.   That, of course, is not so. "This is an action for a wrong.   It is an action for deceit ; for "fraudulently pretending that the defendant's goods were the "plaintiff's goods, and so trying to pass them off.   That is not "a breach of any right of property in the plaintiffs.   It is merely "the exercise by the plaintiff of a right that he has that he "should not be injured by the fraud of the defendant in pre- "tending that the goods manufactured by him, the defendant, "are of the plaintiff's manufacture."   Then, a little later, the Lord Justice proceeds (p. 192-3) :—" I do not understand that "there is any case, or ever has been any case, in which it has "been laid down that a man, who happens to bear a particular "name, is debarred from entering into any trade which he "chooses to enter into merely because there is somebody else of "the same name who has acquired a great reputation in the "manufacture of the particular goods dealt with in this trade. "The truth of the matter is that, inasmuch as the trader who has "established a good business acquires, as I have said, no right "of property in either his own personal name or in the name "by which he chooses to denote his goods, it follows that the "cause of action which the plaintiff has must always be this "action for deceit by the defendant in attempting to pass off his "goods as being the goods of the plaintiff ; and the personal "name of the plaintiff only comes into the matter because the "plaintiff, by the reputation that he has acquired in the busi- "ness, has really come to denote his goods by his own personal "name, just as he might denote them by some fancy name that "he chose to use. . .   A plaintiff never can complain of "the user by the defendant of either the plaintiff's personal "name, or of any other name that he chooses to use for the "purpose of denoting his goods, unless he first establishes that "in his market his goods have come to be known by that name. "It is not a question, as it has been sometimes suggested, of the

" right of the law to restrain a man from using his own name.
" The right and duty of the Court is always to restrain a man
" from using a name that has come to be recognised as the
" name of a particular trader's goods for his, the defendant's,
" goods, so as to suggest that the defendant's goods are the
" plaintiff's goods, and to pass them off as such."

In a subsequent case the right of a real person to use his
real name is distinguished from the right of a registered
company to use, as part of its registered name, the name of
a real person connected with the company. In this case of *Fine
Cotton Spinners Association, Lim. & John Cash & Sons, Lim.
v. Harwood Cash & Co., Lim.* (1907, 2 Ch. 184), the decision
was as follows :—Although, in the absence of fraud or false
representation, a man is entitled to carry on business in his own
name in competition with a similar business previously established under the same name, notwithstanding that confusion
and mistake may arise, yet, *if he has never carried on business
with others*, he cannot, by promoting and registering a company
with a title of which his name forms a part, confer upon that
company the rights which he, as an individual, possesses in the
use of that name.

In a still more recent case this point was further elucidated.
In this case of *Kingston, Miller & Co. Lim. v. Thos. Kingston
& Co. Lim.* (1912, 1 Ch. 575), it appeared that Thomas
Kingston had been in the service of the plaintiff company, of
which his father was managing director. Thomas Kingston
was refused a rise of salary, and left the plaintiff company,
and then helped to promote the defendant company with his
own name as part of their title. The plaintiff company sought
an injunction restraining the defendant company from using
the name they had adopted. The defendant company argued
that Thomas Kingston was entitled to give them the benefit both
of his skill and of his name. The following is a passage from

the judgment (p. 581) :—" There is no doubt that Thomas
" Kingston did, during his service with the plaintiff company,
" acquire qualifications which were of value to himself, in case he
" afterwards started business on his own account, and which
" would be of value to any person who might employ him
" after he had ceased to be employed by the plaintiff company ;
" but he had nothing in the nature of Goodwill. So far as his
" exertions and his skill have contributed to the success of the
" business of the plaintiff company, the advantage of that
" belongs to them. The Goodwill, or that part of their Goodwill
" which is made up of the reputation of Thomas Kingston, is
" their Goodwill, and not his. All that he has is a certain
" personal qualification attaching to the man himself, a quali-
" fication which he may make use of for his own benefit, or
" which he may transfer to somebody else ; but the name is
" not incident to that qualification in the sense that it can be
" transferred to a third person, and give to that third person
" the right to use it regardless of the fact that it may mislead
" the public. In the present case, Thomas Kingston is not
" carrying on business individually, nor is he transferring to the
" defendant company a Goodwill of his own, and as incidental
" to that the right to use his name. What then is the law
" applicable to such a case as the present? I think it is stated
" by Joyce, J., in the case of *Fine Cotton Spinners & Co. v.*
" *Harwood Cash & Co.* (1907, 2 Ch. 184 at p. 190) in the follow-
" ing words :—' I consider as the law stands at present that a
" ' new company with a title of which the name ' A,' for
" ' instance, forms part, has not the natural rights that an
" ' individual born with the name of ' A' would have. I think,
" ' also, that such a company, merely by registration, does not
" ' acquire and incorporate the individual rights which its pro-
" ' moters may respectively have had to carry on business in
" ' their own names ; and, further, I think that a person of the
" ' name of ' A,' without transferring a business and Goodwill

" ' cannot, by merely authorising the promoters of a company, to
" ' use his name as part of their title, confer upon such company
" ' a right to do so as against other people who would be
" ' damaged thereby.' "

We have already said that the same general law applies to the
use of trade names by a registered company and a private individual, subject to the express provisions of the Companies (Consolidation) Act, 1908. The material section of that Act is
Section 63, which enacts that every limited company under the
Act shall paint or affix its name on the outside of every office or
place in which the business of the company is carried on, in a
conspicuous position, in letters easily legible, and shall have its
name mentioned in legible characters in all notices, advertise-
ments, bills, invoices, &c., and imposes penalties for non-
compliance. In two recent cases the effect of the
corresponding sections of the Act of 1862 upon the
use of trade names by a registered company was discussed. In the case of *Pearks, Gunston & Tee, Lim. v.
Thompson, Talmey & Co.* (1901, 18 R.P.C. 185) it appeared
that a person named A. Talmey had carried on business at
certain premises as Talmey & Co., and afterwards assigned
the premises and Goodwill to G., who assigned them to the
plaintiff company. The company continued to carry on the
business as Talmey & Co., although their own name was placed
over the door of the premises. The defendants commenced to
trade as Thompson, Talmey & Co., whereupon the plaintiff
company commenced proceedings against them to restrain them
from using the name Talmey without clearly distinguishing their
business from the plaintiffs' business. The defendants alleged
that the plaintiffs, having used the name Talmey & Co. without
their registered name on their bills and customers' weekly
books, were precluded from suing, as they had by so doing
contravened Section 41 of the Companies Act, 1862. This was
held not to be a good defence, and Mr. Justice Farwell said :—

" I think the defendants are not excused for taking the name
" Talmey, and had no right to do so with the intention of
" acquiring, if they could, some Goodwill from the name of
" Talmey, which belonged to another person. . . . In my
" opinion it is competent for a limited company to acquire
" the Goodwill of a number of properties, and to keep alive
" that Goodwill by keeping the name in such a position, and
" using it in such a way, as to show that they are carrying
" on the trade to which the Goodwill attached which they had
" bought. It is true that they must also comply with the
" Act of Parliament." In a subsequent case of *H. E.
Randall, Lim. v. The British and American Shoe Company*
(1902, 2 Ch. 354) the facts were much the same, except that
the plaintiff company had themselves built up a connection
under the name of " The American Shoe Company," and had
not acquired the benefit of that name by purchase. The action
was to restrain the defendants from carrying on a business
similar to the plaintiff company's business under a name so
similar as to deprive them of their connection. The action was
successful, and the Judge said :—" Although at all shops of
" ' The American Shoe Company ' the words H. E. Randall,
" Lim., proprietors, have appeared conspicuously over the door
" for a considerable time past, they do not appear to have
" attracted much attention, and many persons were unaware that
" the plaintiffs were the proprietors of the American Shoe Com-
" pany. The argument addressed to me was that if the plain-
" tiffs had bought an old business, and carried it on under
" the old name exactly without their own, they might have
" obtained protection for it, but as the plaintiffs did not purchase
" an existing business, but by their exertions have created and
" made famous the name, reputation, and business of the
" American Shoe Company, the latter have been unlawfully
" acquired, and are not entitled to protection. I am of opinion
" that no such distinction can be established between a business

" bought and a business created and established.   The Com-
" panies Act, 1862, Sections 41 and 42, imposes certain
" penalties on a company for non-compliance with its provi-
" sions ; but the additional penalty of forfeiting its Goodwill
" to any dishonest person who chooses to steal it is not imposed
" by the statute."

CHAPTER III.

TRADE MARKS AND THEIR PROTECTION.

TRADE marks, unlike trade names, are now the subject of statutory regulations, but before we pass to the definition of a trade mark, which is contained in the Trade Marks Act, 1905, let us look at some definitions contained in decided cases. Bacon, V.C., in *Ransome v. Graham* (1882, 51 L.J. Ch. 897), said :—" The law relating to trade marks has been established " by decisions extending over centuries, and although its applica- " tion has been somewhat modified by recent statutes relating " to trade marks, and thereby adapted more conveniently to " modern usages, the law has undergone no change in its " essential principle. That principle may be stated thus : a " manufacturer who produces an article of merchandise which " he announces as one of public utility, and who places upon it a " mark, by which it is distinguished from all other articles of a " similar kind, with the intention that it may be known to be of " his manufacture, becomes the exclusive owner of that which is " thenceforth called his trade mark. By the law of this country, " and the like law prevails in most other civilised countries, he " obtains a property in the mark which he so affixes to his goods. " The property thus acquired by the manufacturer, like all other " property, is under the protection of the law, and for the " invasion of the right of the owner of such property the law " affords a remedy similar in all respects to that by which the " possession and enjoyment of all property is secured to the " owners."

The word "manufacture" is a convenient word to use, but there may be cases in which a trade mark distinguishes not the manufacture, but the selection, or some other operation upon the goods. This is recognised in the definition given of the meaning of a trade mark in the case of *In re Australian Wines, Lim.* (1889, 41 Ch.D. 278) :—"What does a trade mark mean? " It means the mark under which a particular individual trades, " and which indicates the goods to be his goods—either goods "manufactured by him, or goods selected by him, or goods " which in some way or other pass through his hands in the " course of trade. That is the meaning of a trade mark. It is " a mode of designating goods as being the goods which have " been, in some way or other, dealt with by A. B., the person " who owns the trade mark."

In the case of *Major Bros. v. Franklin & Sons* (1908, 1 K.B. 712) it was held that a trade mark might be registered in connection with vegetables and other natural products of the earth ; and that a salesman on commission might be the proprietor of a trade mark in respect of the goods which he sold on commission.

To this we may add what Bowen, L.J., called, in the case of *In re Powell's Trade Mark* (1893, 2 Ch. 388), the simplest consideration of what is really the function of a trade mark :—" The " function of a trade mark is to give an indication to the pur- " chaser, or possible purchaser, as to the manufacture or quality " of the goods—to give an indication to his eye of the trade " source from which the goods come, or the trade hands through " which they pass on their way to the market. It tells the " person who is about to buy, or considering whether he shall " buy, that what is presented to him is either what he has known " before under the similar name as coming from a source with " which he is acquainted, or that it is what he has heard of as " coming from that similar source. It is obvious that if it is to " be an indication to the purchaser's eye of what I have stated,

" it must either be impressed on the goods or so accompany the
" goods as to produce that effect upon the purchaser," and this
extract from the judgment of James, L.J., in *Massam v.
Thorley's Cattle Food Co.* (1880, 14 Ch.D. 748) :—" The
" words Thorley's Food for Cattle would, according to my view
" of the case, indicate to a purchaser this, 'You have always
" ' had a very good article called Thorley's Food for Cattle ; if
" ' any article bears that name, that is to you a guarantee that
" ' it comes from the same place from which that has come with
" ' which you have hitherto been well satisfied.' That, in truth,
" is the meaning, and object, and result of a trade mark. It
" indicates this, that you may take this as a warranty that it has
" come from the particular manufacturer of the goods with
" which you have been hitherto pleased."

A trade mark was not at once recognised as property. " For
" many years nobody ever supposed that you could assign a
" trade mark at all. For many years a trade mark was only
" put in evidence as one of the pieces of evidence which might
" tend to show that a defendant was selling as and for the
" goods of the plaintiff goods which were not the goods of
" the plaintiff. But gradually the trade mark obtained more
" and more importance in such discussions, until Lord Westbury
" surprised the profession by asserting that there might be pro-
" perty in a trade mark." (*Pinto v. Badman*, 1891, 8 R.P.C.
187.) Lord Westbury laid down this new principle in the case
of the *Leather Cloth Co., Lim. v The American Leather Cloth
Co., Lim.* (1865, 4 De Gex, J. & S. 137) :—" The representation
" which the defendant is supposed to make that his goods are
" the goods of another person is not actually made otherwise
" than by his appropriating or using the trade mark which such
" other person has an exclusive right to use in connection with
" the sale of some commodity, and if the plaintiff has an exclu-
" sive right so to use any particular mark or symbol it becomes
" his property for the purposes of such application, and the act

" of the defendant is a violation of such right of property,
" corresponding with the piracy of copyright, or the infringe-
" ment of a patent.   I cannot therefore assent to the dictum that
" there is no property in a trade mark. . . . The true
" principle therefore would seem to be that the jurisdiction of
" the Court in the protection given to trade marks rests upon
" property, and that the Court interferes by injunction, because
" that is the only mode by which property of this description
" can be effectually protected."   In a subsequent case, *Hall v.
Barrows* (1865, 4 De Gex, J. & S. 151), Lord Westbury said :—
" Imposition on the public is indeed necessary for the plain-
" tiff's title, but in this way only, that it is the test of the
" invasion by the defendant of the plaintiff's right of property ;
" for there is no injury if the mark used by the defendant is not
" such as is mistaken, or is likely to be mistaken, by the public
" for the mark of the plaintiff ; but the true ground of this
" Court's jurisdiction is property, and the necessity of interfer-
" ing to protect it by reason of the inadequacy of the legal
" remedy."

For a further discussion of the question of " property " in
common law trade marks (with which Lord Westbury was dealing), and in registered trade marks, see the case of *A. J.
Spalding & Bros. v. A. W. Gamage, Lim.* at p. 37 below.

It is evident from what has been just said that at Common
Law the right to a trade mark depended on user of the trade mark.
As counsel put it in the course of argument in the case cited
immediately below :—" Before the Trade Marks Act 1875,
" trade marks had become general in this country, but, as the
" law then stood, a trader who had adopted a trade mark was
" subject to several disadvantages in obtaining the protection of
" the Court. He had to prove that his mark had become
" identified with his goods ; he could acquire no right to the
" mark except by considerable user ; and he had no means of

"ascertaining whether the same mark was already in use by "somebody else."

The Act of 1875 was passed to deal with this state of the law, and its general aim was described by Lord Parker in giving judgment in the case of *Registrar of Trade Marks v. W. & G. Du Cros, Lim.* (1913, A.C. 624) in the following passage :— "The scheme of the Act of 1875 was not, as it might have "been, to create a register of all common law marks. On the "contrary, the Act specifies *certain kinds of marks* (somewhat "limited in number), which the legislature considered appro- "priate for use as trade marks, and allowed anyone, *without* "*any previous user thereof,* to apply for the registration of any "mark of a kind specified, making registration equivalent to "user, and granting the registered proprietor a monopoly."

The registration of Trade Marks which was begun in 1875 has been continued since under a series of Trade Mark Acts, the one now in force being the Trade Marks Act, 1905, which came into force on April 1, 1906. This Act is given in full in Appendix A.

On April 1st 1920 fresh legislation, viz. the Trade Marks Act 1919, came into operation. Part I of this Act provides for the registration of certain trade marks not registrable under the principal Act of 1905. From April 1st 1920 the register of Trade Marks will consist of two parts. In Part A will be found all trade marks entered in the old register under the principal Act of 1905, and all trade marks which after April 1st 1920 may be registered under the Act of 1905. In Part B will be found all trade marks registered under the Act of 1919. Marks registrable under Part B are not "certain kinds of marks," but *all lawful marks.* On the other hand, *not less than two years bonâ fide use of the mark* in the United Kingdom *must be proved,* and *the mark must be capable* of *distinguishing the goods of the applicant.* In other words, Part B is mainly a register of trade marks, which we call elsewhere Common Law Trade Marks, and the scheme of the new Act is to give persons the option of registering all common law marks which have been in use for two years.   Part II of the Act of 1919 is concerned with the prevention of abuses where the name of a patented article has been registered as its trade mark, or where the application is to register the name of some chemical substance.   Part III of the Act of 1919 contains detailed amendments of the Act of 1905.   The Act of 1919 will also be found in full in Appendix A.   The following notes are explanatory of the more important sections of these two Acts.

The definition of a trade mark for the purposes of the Act of 1905 is merely a convenient summary of the previous common law decisions on the point.

First of all, the Act defines a mark as including a device, brand, heading, label, ticket, name, signature, word, letter, numeral, or any combination thereof.   It then proceeds :—" A " ' trade mark ' shall mean a mark used, or proposed to be used " upon or in connection with goods for the purpose of indicating " that they are the goods of the proprietor of such trade mark " by virtue of manufacture, selection, certification, dealing with, " or offering for sale."

Section 8 of the Trade Marks Act, 1905, also re-affirms a common law principle.   We have seen that a trade name is limited to the owner's business, and that Jones, who sells butter, cannot complain of another man, whether really named Jones or not, who sells pianos under the name of Jones.   The common law applied the same principle to trade marks.   In *Hall v. Barrows* (1865, 4 De Gex. J & S. 151) it was said :—" An " ironfounder, who uses a particular mark for his manufactures " in iron, could not restrain the use of the same mark when " impressed on cotton or woollen goods."

Accordingly, the Trade Marks Act, 1905, enacts in Section **8** that a trade mark must be registered in respect of particular goods, or classes of goods. Where the class of goods for registration purposes is a wide one, the trade mark will only apply to the kinds of goods which are dealt with by the owner, and in connection with which it is actually used, even if they only comprise part of the registration class. In the case of *Edwards v. Dennis* (1885, 30 Ch.D. 454) the assignor of a trade mark had registered his mark under the Trade Marks Registry Act, 1875, in respect of the entire class of goods falling under the head of unwrought and partly wrought metals used in manufacture. His only business actually was that of a manufacturer of galvanised iron sheets. He sold the Goodwill of his business and the trade mark. The assignee brought an action to restrain the defendant from using his trade mark on steel wire and iron wire, which came in the same registration class of unwrought and partly wrought metals. He was not successful, and Fry, L.J., said :—" I do express my opinion that under " the 2nd section no trade mark can be assigned except in " connection with the Goodwill of the business in which it has " been used, which business must be co-extensive with the " goods, or classes of goods, in respect of which the trade mark " is registered. The result therefore is that if a person registers " a trade mark in respect of goods in which he carries on no " business, he does so at his peril, and an assignee has no " exclusive right to a trade mark unless the assignment is of a " business co-extensive with the trade mark as registered. In " the present case Mr. Edwards claims that under his assign- " ment he became entitled to the exclusive use of the trade mark " in respect of the entire class of goods falling under the head " of unwrought and partly wrought metals used in manufacture, " whereas the Goodwill assigned was only that of the business " of manufacturing galvanised iron sheets. Consequently the " assignment did not extend to the entire class."

Section 9 of the Act of 1905 is the section which specifies in detail the kind of marks which are considered suitable for registration in what is now called Part A of the Register.   As amended by the Act of 1919 it enacts as follows :—

" A registrable trade mark must contain or consist of at least " one of the following essential particulars :—

(1) The name of a company, individual, or firm represented in a special and particular manner.

(2) The signature of the applicant for registration, or some predecessor in his business.

(3) An invented word or words.

(4) A word or words having no direct reference to the character or quality of the goods, and not being, according to its ordinary signification, a geographical name or a surname.

(5) Any other distinctive mark, but a name, signature, or word, or words, other than such as fall within the descriptions in the above paragraphs (1), (2), (3), and (4) shall not be registrable under the provisions of this paragraph except upon evidence of its distinctiveness.

" Provided always that any special or distinctive word or " words, letter, numeral, or combination of letters or numerals " used as a trade mark by the applicant or his predecessors in " business before 13th August 1875 which has continued to be " used (either in its original form or with additions or alterations " not substantially affecting the identity of the same) down to " the date of the application for registration shall be registrable " as a trade mark under this Act.

" For the purpose of this section ' distinctive ' shall mean " adapted to distinguish the goods of the proprietor of the trade " mark from those of other persons.

"In determining whether a trade mark is so adapted, the "tribunal may, in the case of a trade mark in actual use, take "into consideration the extent to which such user has rendered "such trade mark in fact distinctive for the goods with respect "to which it is registered or proposed to be registered."

Some of these classes explain themselves, and certain general principles have now been settled as to the conditions under which the use of names, both of things, persons, and places, will be allowed to be registered as trade marks.

First as to the use of the name of a new article. In the case of *In re an Application by Williams, Lim.* (1917, 34 R.P.C. 197), the question involved was whether "Chocaroons" could be registered as a trade mark for a new sweetmeat of the same class as chocolate macaroons. Warrington, L.J., said the crucial question was : "Is the word a mark used or proposed "to be used upon or in connection with goods for the purpose "of indicating that they are the goods of the proprietor of the "mark, or is it rather used or proposed to be used to denominate "a particular kind of goods, and to distinguish them from other "goods comprised with them in a class of a more or less compre- "hensive nature." He then proceeds to quote from the judgment of Mr. J. Parker (afterwards Lord Parker) in the "Diabolo" case *In re Philippart's Trade Mark* (1908, 25 R.P.C. at p. 572) :—"It seems to me that a person who is advertising or "bringing on the market under a particular name a game which "everyone has a right to sell, and is at the same time marking "part of the apparatus with the name of the game, can hardly "be said to be using the mark for the purpose of distinguish- "ing his own goods from those of other manufacturers, and "similarly an intention to use the name as the name of the "game seems to me to be inconsistent with any *bonâ fide* inten- "tion to use it as a distinguishing mark for his own goods." His Lordship continued—"So in the present case, if the evi- "dence establishes that the applicants have brought into the

"market a new sweetmeat under the name 'Chocaroons'—a
"sweetmeat which other people may make—that name cannot
"be said to be used for the purpose of distinguishing their
"goods from those of others, but is used for the purpose of
"distinguishing the particular sweetmeat from other sweet-
"meats, and, if so, is not a trade mark within the definition
"and ought not to be registered." Finally, he points out that
"the danger of allowing the name given to a new article to be
"registered as a trade mark is that the article may become
"known and popular under that name, and other persons,
"though they may have a right to make and sell the article, are
"practically debarred from doing so, because the public would
"refuse to buy it unless sold under the name by which they
"know it. The owner of the trade mark may thus obtain a
"monopoly in the goods by having the exclusive right to use
"the name."

The provisions of item 5 in Section 9 were explained by
Fletcher Moulton, L.J., in the case of *Joseph Crosfield & Son's
Application* (L.R. 1910, 1 Ch. 130, at p. 144):—"To my
"mind these provisions are chiefly directed to remedy the well-
"known defects in the working of the previous legislation. In
"the first place the exclusion of words under that legislation was
"by whole classes. But though it may be desirable in general
"to exclude from registration words of a particular class, it
"by no means follows that every individual word in that class
"would be objectionable as a trade mark in the case of every
"kind of goods. For example, few would doubt the desir-
"ability of excluding geographical terms as a class. But if,
"as suggested during the argument, a trader desired to register
"'Monte Rosa' for cigarettes, or 'Teneriffe' for boiler plates,
"no practical inconvenience would arise from his doing so.
"The second defect was more difficult to remedy, but on the
"other hand it affected cases that had a strong claim on the
"merits. It often occurs in trade that by continued use words

" get recognised as denoting the goods of a particular firm.
" The words may in themselves be unsuitable to be chosen as
" trade marks, but they have, in fact, become so. The oft
" quoted case of Yorkshire Relish is one example of this, and
" the words Worcester Sauce would almost certainly have been
" another example had the original maker of the article exer-
" cised due vigilance in protecting their rights. Apart from
" the Trade Marks Act there would be nothing to prevent such
" words becoming trade marks in the eye of the law, and it was
" an obvious defect in the earlier legislation that it failed to
" give the benefits of registration to such marks when they had
" become duly established. The present Act seems to remedy
" these defects by abandoning the policy of absolute exclusion
" of all the members of specified classes of words and substitut-
" ing therefor a judicial examination of the merits of each par-
" ticular case, and leaving the Court free to pronounce the word
" or words to be eligible for registration if on such examination
" it holds it proper to do so."

The application of these principles is illustrated by the following cases :—

In the case of *Teofani Lim. v. A. Teofani* (1913, 30 R.P.C.
446), Swinfen Eady, L.J. (at p. 464) said :—" Caution is neces-
" sary in admitting surnames to registration, and the circum-
" stances in which registration should be allowed are exceptional.
" Much would depend on the name itself, whether it is a sur-
" name of unusual occurrence in the United Kingdom, or
" whether it is a name not infrequently met with ; and again,
" whether the application is made after the word has been in
" use as a trade mark for some time, and there is evidence of
" distinctiveness acquired by user, or whether the application
" refers to a mark ' proposed to be used ' but not yet in actual
" use."

The name Teofani being very uncommon, and its user for 20
years having in fact made it distinctive for cigarettes, it was

allowed to be registered.   On the same principles " Daimler "
(1913, 33 R.P.C. 337) and " Muratti " (1915, 32 R.P.C. 77)
were passed for registration.   Coming to British names, we
may note that Cadbury has been passed (1915, 1 Ch. 331), and
Crawford has been rejected (1917, 34 R.P.C. 94), but it should
be noted that the Cadbury application was in respect of confec-
tionery, and that in respect of chocolate, &c. it had already
been on the register for a long period, so that it was difficult to
say that a name which they had used as a trade mark, or had
upon the register as their trade mark for a great number of
years, was not adapted to distinguish their goods from the goods
of other dealers.

Very recently the name Lodge has been allowed to be registered in connection with sparking plugs, and the name Avery in
connection with weighing apparatus.

Another new provision, so far as statute law is concerned, is
contained in Section 11, which enacts that " it shall not be
" lawful to register as a trade mark. or part of a trade mark, any
" matter, the use of which would by reason of its being calcu-
" lated to deceive or otherwise be disentitled to protection in a
" Court of Justice, or would be contrary to law or morality, or
" any scandalous design."   The principle which underlies the
rule as to not allowing a mark calculated to deceive to be registered was laid down by the Judges a long time ago.

In the case of the *Leather Cloth Co., Lim. v. The American
Leather Cloth Co.* (1865. 4 De Gex. J. & S. 137), which we have
already quoted as to property in a trade mark, this principle is
thus laid down and illustrated.   Lord Westbury said :—" It is
" essential that the plaintiff should not in his trade mark, or in
" the business connected with it, be himself guilty of any false or
" misleading misrepresentation.   The question then arises, what
" amounts to a material false representation?"   After discussing the handing down from partnership to partnership of the

original trade name, Lord Westbury proceeded :—" But suppose
" an individual or firm to have gained credit for a particular
" manufacture, and that the goods are marked and stamped in
" such a way as to denote that they are made by such person or
" firm, and that the name has gained currency and credit in the
" market (there being no secret process or invention), could such
" person or firm, on ceasing to carry on business, sell and assign
" the right to use such name and mark to another firm carrying
" on the same business in another place? Suppose a firm of
" A. B. & Co. to have been clothiers in Wiltshire for fifty years,
" and that broadcloth marked ' A. B. & Co., makers, Wilts,' has
" obtained great reputation in the market, and that A. B. & Co.,
" on discontinuing business, sell and transfer the right to use
" their name and mark to a firm of C. D. & Co., who are
" clothiers in Yorkshire, would the latter be protected by a Court
" of Equity in their claim to an exclusive right to use the name
" and mark of A. B. & Co. ?   I am of opinion that no such pro-
" tection ought to be given.   It is true that a name, or the style
" of a firm, may by long usage become a mere trade mark, and
" cease to convey any representation as to the fact of the person
" who makes, or the place of manufacture; but *where any*
" *symbol or label claimed as a trade mark is so constructed or*
" *worded as to make or contain a distinct assertion which is*
" *false, I think no property can be claimed on it; or, in other*
" *words, the right to the exclusive use of it cannot be main-*
" *tained.''*   (See also the case of *Thorniloe v. Hill, supra* p. 4.)

The method of registration is dealt with in Sections 12 to 18
of the Act of 1905, and Sections 28 to 31 provide for the
renewal of registration after a period of 14 years from the date
of the original registration.

By Section 40 registration is made *primâ facie* evidence of
the validity of the trade mark, and by Section 41 registration,
after the expiration of seven years from the date of original

registration, is to be conclusive evidence of validity unless such original registration was obtained by fraud, or unless the trade mark offends against the provisions of Section 11.

The combined effect of Sections 11 and 41 has been the subject of some doubt. The words in it which have been the subject of controversy are the words "or otherwise be disentitled to protection" following the words "calculated to deceive," and preceding the words "contrary to law or morality or any scandalous design." In the case of *In re Imperial Tobacco Co.'s Trade Mark* (1918, 35 R.P.C., p. 185), it was held that Section 11 must be a prohibition to register something which, but for the prohibition, might have been registered, and that the words "or otherwise be disentitled to protection" were confined to reasons similar to those explicitly stated in the section. In other words, if a trade mark complies with Section 9, but does not comply with Section 11 because it is deceptive, or seditious, or immoral, or scandalous, then it ought not to be registered, and, if registered, it can at any time be removed from the register, even though seven years have elapsed since its registration. On the other hand, if a trade mark does not comply with Section 9, *e.g.*, if it is not distinctive of the owner's goods, but by inadvertence it is registered, then if it is allowed to stay on the register for 7 years, it cannot afterwards be removed.

The only other section material for our purpose is Section 45, which enacts that "nothing in this Act contained shall be "deemed to affect rights of action against any person for pass-"ing off goods as those of another person, or the remedies in "respect thereof."

Passing off goods as those of another person may be effected either by the use of a name for the business which resembles the name of a well-known business, or by the use of a name for the goods which resembles the name of well-known goods. The use of a business name has already been dealt with, so that we need only consider the use of a deceptive name for goods. These cases arise where the trade name for the goods cannot be registered as a trade mark, and such unregistered trade names are sometimes spoken of as common law trade marks.

In a recent case taken to the House of Lords, *Reddaway v. Banham* (1896, A.C. 199), Lord Herschell adopted the principle laid down by Lord Kingsdown in the *Leather Cloth Co. v. American Leather Cloth Co.* :—" The fundamental rule is that " one man has no right to put off his goods for sale as the goods " of a rival trader, and he cannot therefore be allowed to use " names, marks, letters, or other indicia, by which he may " induce purchasers to believe that the goods which he is selling " are the manufacture of another person." Lord Herschell proceeded :—" It is, in my opinion, this fundamental rule which " governs all cases, whatever be the particular mode adopted by " any man for putting off his goods as those of a rival trader, " whether it is done by the use of a mark which has become his " trade mark, or in any other way." The actual decision in this case, which is a very strong one, is given in the headnote :—" A trader is not entitled to pass off his goods as the " goods of another trader by selling them under a name which " is likely to deceive purchasers (whether immediate or " ultimate) into the belief that they are buying the goods of that " other trader, although in its primary meaning the name is " merely a true description of the goods. The plaintiff had for " some years made belting, and sold it as ' Camel Hair Belting,' " *a name which had come to mean in the trade the plaintiff's* " *belting, and nothing else.* The defendant began to sell belt- " ing made of the yarn of camels' hair, and stamped it ' Camel " Hair Belting,' so as to be likely to mislead purchasers into the " belief that it was the plaintiff's belting, endeavouring thus to " pass off his goods as the plaintiff's. Held, that the plaintiff " was entitled to an injunction restraining the defendant from " using the words ' camel hair ' as descriptive of, or in connec-

"tion with, belting made, or sold, or offered for sale by him, and
"not manufactured by the plaintiff, without clearly distinguish-
"ing such belting from the plaintiff's belting, or from describing
"his belting so as to represent or induce the belief that it was
"the plaintiff's belting." Lord Herschell also approved of
the previous decision of the House of Lords in *Wotherspoon v.
Currie* (1872, 5 H.L. 508), where the plaintiff had for many
years manufactured starch at Glenfield, and sold it as Glenfield
starch, and was granted an injunction against a rival trader who
had moved to Glenfield for the purpose of being able to describe
his starch as Glenfield starch. As to the argument that in both
these cases the defendants were only telling the truth as to their
goods, Lord Herschell said :—" I think the fallacy lies in over-
"looking the fact that a word may acquire in a trade a secon-
"dary signification differing from its primary one, and that if it
"is used to persons in the trade who will understand it, and be
"known and intended to understand it in its secondary sense,
"it will none the less be a falsehood that in its primary sense it
"may be true." Then, on the general principle, Lord Herschell
further said :—" What right, it was asked, can an individual
"have to restrain another from using a common English word
"because he has chosen to employ it as his trade mark? I
"answer he has no such right ; but he has a right to insist that
"it shall not be used without explanation or qualification if such
"a case would be an instrument of fraud." But where the
descriptive term is an ordinary English word it must be clearly
proved that it has acquired a secondary or special meaning, so
as to denote only the goods of the plaintiff. In the case of the
Cellular Clothing Co. v. Manton (1899, A.C. 326), the House
of Lords held that "cellular cloth" had not acquired such a
secondary meaning.

In the same way the House of Lords held recently in the case
of *Horlick's Malted Milk Co. v. Summerskill* (1917, 34 R.P.C.
63), that the expression "malted milk" was not a fancy name

of the appellants' goods, but merely descriptive, and they were not, therefore, entitled to the exclusive use of it.

Where an article, though originally invented by one man, has come to be manufactured by several people, no one can acquire a monopoly in the use of the name. Thus in the case of *Condy v. Mitchell* (1877, 37 L.T.N.S. 766) it was admitted by the plaintiff that the words "Condy's Fluid" did not import that the article sold had been manufactured by Mr. Condy, but simply imported that a particular article, which might be manufactured either by Condy, or the defendants, or by any other member of the public, was offered for sale to the public, that article being made of a certain composition. So in the case of *Liebig's Extract of Meat Co. v. Hanbury* (1867, 17 L.T.N.S. 298), the plaintiffs having got Liebig to assist them, and lend them his name, sought to prevent the defendants from selling anything under the name of "Liebig's Extract of Meat." The answer was that Liebig's extract of meat had ceased to be a thing made by Liebig, because Liebig had published to the world the mode by which it was made, and it had been made and manufactured, and had got into the Pharmacopœia and into books of cookery, and had become as much known as if it were simply called "extract of meat," and had therefore ceased to have any connection with Liebig as the maker of it for the purpose of the manufacture.

The usual passing off action is an action by A against B because B is passing off his goods as A's goods. A novel point was decided in the case of *A. G. Spalding & Bros. v. A. W. Gamage, Lim.* (1915, 32 R.P.C. 273). In that case it appeared that Gamages had obtained a large number of footballs manufactured by Spaldings, but sold off by them to make way for a superior pattern. Gamages were passing off the inferior footballs as if they were footballs of this new superior pattern. Spaldings obtained an injunction restraining Gamages from

such passing off, and at the hearing, on appeal to the House of
Lords, Lord Parker took the opportunity of explaining the
different theories on which passing off actions have been based.
He said (p. 283) :—" The action in which the appeal arises is
" what is known as a passing off action, and having regard to
" the arguments which have been addressed to your Lordships, I
" think it well to say a few words as to the principle on which
" such actions are founded.   The principle is stated by Turner,
" L.J., in *Burgess v. Burgess* (1853, 3 de G.M. & G. 896),
" and by Lord Halsbury in *Reddaway v. Banham* (L.R. 1906,
" A.C. at p. 204), in the proposition that nobody has any right
" to *represent* his goods as the goods of somebody else.   It is
" also sometimes stated in the proposition that nobody has the
" right to pass off his goods as the goods of somebody else.   I
" prefer the former statement, for whatever doubts may be
" suggested in the earlier authorities, it has long been settled
" that actual passing off of a defendant's goods for the plaintiffs
" need not be proved as a condition precedent to relief in equity,
" either by way of injunction, or of an enquiry as to profits or
" damages.   Nor need the representation be fraudulently made.
" It is enough that it has in fact been made, whether fraudu-
" lently or otherwise, and that damages may probably ensue,
" though the complete innocence of the party making it may be
" a reason for limiting the account of profits to the period
" subsequent to the date at which he becomes aware of the true
" facts. . . .   The proposition that no one has a right to
" represent his goods as the goods of somebody else   must, I
" think, as has been assumed in this case, involve as a corollary
" the further proposition that no one who has in his hands
" the goods of another of a particular class or quality has a
" right to represent these goods to be the goods of that other of
" a different quality, or belonging to a different class. . . .
" There appears to be considerable diversity of opinion as to
" the nature of the right, the invasion of which is the subject

" of what are known as passing off actions. The more general
" opinion appears to be that the right is a right of property.
" This view naturally demands an answer to the question—
" property in what?   Some authorities say property in the mark,
" name or get up improperly used by the defendant.   Others
" say, property in the business or Goodwill likely to be injured
" by the misrepresentation.   Lord Herschell in *Reddaway v.*
" *Banham* expressly dissents from the former view ; and if the
" right invaded is a right of property at all, there are, I think,
" strong reasons for preferring the latter view.   In the first
" place, cases of misrepresentation by the use of a mark, name,
" or get up do not exhaust all possible cases of misrepresentation.
"   .   .   .   Further, it is extremely difficult to see how a man
" can be said to have property in descriptive words such as
" ' Camel Hair ' in the case of *Reddaway v. Banham*, where
" every trader is entitled to use the words, provided only he uses
" them in such a way as not to be calculated to deceive.   Even
" in the case of what are sometimes referred to as Common Law
" trade marks, the property, if any, of the so-called owner, is
" in its nature transitory, and only exists so long as the mark
" is distinctive of his goods in the eyes of the public or a class
" of the public.   Indeed, the necessity of proving this distinc-
" tiveness in each case as a step in the proof of the false repre-
" sentation relied on, was one of the evils sought to be reme-
" died by the Trade Marks Act, 1875, which conferred a real
" right of property on the owner of a registered trade mark.
" I had to consider the matter in the case of *Burberrys v.*
" *Cording* (1909, 26 R.P.C. 693), and I came to the same
" conclusion."

We now come to the new provisions of the Act of 1919, as
apart from mere amendments made in the Act of 1905.

Under Section 2, where any mark has for not less than two
years been *bonâ fide* used in the United Kingdom upon or in
connection with any goods (whether for sale in the United

Kingdom or exportation abroad) for the purpose of indicating that they are the goods of the proprietor of the mark by virtue of manufacture, selection, certification, dealing with or offering for sale, the person claiming to be the proprietor of the mark may apply in writing to the registrar in the prescribed manner to have the mark entered as his registered trade mark in Part B of the register in respect of such goods.

The registrar shall consider every such application for registration of a trade mark in Part B of the register, and if it appears to him, after such search, if any, as he may deem necessary, that the application is inconsistent with the provisions of Section 11 or Section 19 of the Act of 1905, or if he is not satisfied that the mark has been so used as aforesaid, or that it is capable of distinguishing the goods of the applicant, he may refuse the application, or may accept it subject to conditions, amendments or modifications as to the goods or classes of goods in respect of which the mark is to be registered, or to such limitations, if any, as to mode or place of user or otherwise as he may think right to impose, and in any other case he shall accept the application.   Every such application shall be accompanied by a statutory declaration verifying the user, including the date of first user, and such date shall be entered on the register.

Any such refusal or conditional acceptance shall be subject to appeal to the Court, and, if the ground for refusal is insufficiency of evidence as to user, such refusal shall be without prejudice to any application for registration of the trade mark in Part A of the register.

A mark may be registered in Part B notwithstanding any registration in Part A by the same proprietor of the same mark.   The registration of a person as the proprietor of a trade mark in Part B of the register shall be *primâ facie* evidence that that person has the exclusive right to the use of that trade mark, but, in any action for infringement of a trade mark entered in Part B of the register, no injunction, interdict, or other relief shall be granted to the owner of the trade mark in respect of such registration, if the defendant establishes to the satisfaction of the Court that the user, of which the plaintiff complains, is not calculated to deceive or to lead to the belief that the goods, the subject of such user, were goods manufactured, selected, certified, dealt with, or offered for sale by the proprietor of the trade mark.

In general, the provisions of the Act of 1905 are made applicable to applications for registration under the Act of 1919, and the exceptions will be found in the first schedule to the Act of 1919. Certain provisions of the Act of 1905 had obviously to be excluded as being inconsistent with the scheme of the Act of 1919, e.g., the classifications of registrable trade marks (Section 9) and the making of registration conclusive after seven years (Section 41).

If a person applies for the registration of a trade mark in Part A of the register under the Act of 1905, and it is intimated to him that his application will be unsuccessful (e.g., because his mark does not comply with Section 9), the registrar may, with the applicant's consent, instead of refusing the application, treat it as an application for registration in Part B of the register. But, of course, two years' user, as defined above, must be proved.

The provisions of Part II of the Act of 1919 as to trade marks which are names of articles are as follows :—

Where in the case of an article or substance manufactured under any patent in force at or granted after the passing of the Act, a word trade mark registered in Part A or Part B of the register is the name or only practicable name of the article or substance so manufactured, all rights to the exclusive use of such trade mark, whether under the common law, or by registration (and notwithstanding the provisions of Section 41 of the Act of 1905) shall cease upon the expiration of the patent, and thereafter such word shall not be deemed a distinctive mark, and may be removed by the Court from the register on the application of any person aggrieved.

Further, no word which is the only practicable name or description of any single chemical element or single chemical compound, as distinguished from a mixture, shall be registered as a trade mark, and any such word now or hereafter in the register may, notwithstanding Section 41 of the Act of 1905, he removed by the Court from the register on the application of any person aggrieved, but this provision is not to apply where the mark is used to denote only the proprietor's brand or make of such substance, as distinguished from the substance as made by others, and in association with a suitable and practicable name open to the public use.　Marks of this kind registered before the passing of the Act of 1919 are to have four years' grace from the passing of the Act.

CHAPTER IV.

THE NATURE OF GOODWILL.

WE may now proceed to a more detailed consideration of the nature of Goodwill as defined by the Courts. The term is a commercial rather than a legal one, and for the most part the Judges have been content to take such a definition of Goodwill as would suffice for the fair settlement of the particular dispute before them. We must not expect therefore too much in the way of precision. It is also true that "it is only recently that the "importance of Goodwill, and the necessity of preventing its "improper appropriation, have been fully recognised." (*In re David & Mathews*, 1899, 1 Ch. 378.) We may therefore expect a greater degree of incompleteness in the earlier than in the later decisions.

The earliest case is *Crutwell v. Lye* (1810, 17 Ves. 335). Here Lord Eldon said :—" The Goodwill which has been the subject "of sale is nothing more than the probability that the old "customers will resort to the old place." This description, insufficient to comprise every form of what is now ordinarily understood as Goodwill, is, as might be expected, accurate enough to describe the Goodwill of the class of business to which Lord Eldon's mind was directed—viz., that of a country wagoner. It is not the name nor the personality of the driver, but the place whence he starts and the probability that those who take their goods thither will find a carriage for them which form the value of such a business. Lord Herschell, in the recent case of *Trego v. Hunt*, decided in the House of Lords in 1895

(L.R. 1896, A.C. 7), said :—" If the language of Lord Eldon is " to be taken as a definition of general application, I think it is " far too narrow, and I am not satisfied that it was intended by " Lord Eldon as an exhaustive definition."

In the case of *England v. Downs* (1843, 6 Beav. 269) Goodwill was stated to consist of the chance or probability that custom will be had at a certain place of business in consequence of the way in which that business has been previously carried out. Such a Goodwill practically consists of the good reputation of a business.

The next case in point of time was one dealing with the Goodwill of a solicitor's business, but it will be more convenient to group together the cases dealing with professions, so we will pass on to the case of *Churton v. Douglas* (1859, 28 L.J. Ch. 841), which related to a Bradford stuff merchant's business. Here the nature of Goodwill was fully considered by Vice-Chancellor Wood. Referring to *Crutwell v. Lye* (*supra*), the Vice-Chancellor said :—" It is said that Lord Eldon has plainly " laid down . . . . that Goodwill *simpliciter* carries no " more with it than the advantage which is possessed by occupy" ing the premises which were occupied by the former firm, and " the chance which is thereby given of the customers being " attracted to those premises. It is rather too narrow a view of " what is laid down by Lord Eldon there to say that it is con" fined to that. Goodwill, I apprehend, must mean every advan" tage—affirmative advantage, if I may so express it, as con" trasted with the negative advantage of the vendor not carrying " on the business himself—that has been acquired by the old " firm by carrying on its business, everything connected with the " premises, and the name of the firm, and everything connected " with or carrying with it the benefit of the business. . . . " It would be absurd, as it seems to me, to say that when a large " wholesale business is conducted the public are mindful whether " it is carried on at one end of the Strand or the other, or in

" Fleet Street, or in the Strand, or any place adjoining, and that
" they regard that, and do not regard the identity of the house
" of business—namely, the firm. . . . And when a person
" parts with the Goodwill of a business, he means to part with
" all that good disposition which customers entertain towards his
" particular shop or house of business, and which may induce
" them to continue their custom with it."

In the case of *Ginesi v. Cooper & Co.* (1880, 14 Ch.D. 599),
Sir George Jessel was dealing with the sale of the Goodwill of a
stone merchant's business. He said :—" Attracting customers to
" the business is a matter connected with the carrying of it on.
" It is the formation of that connection which has made the
" value of the thing that the late firm sold, and they really had
" nothing else to sell in the shape of Goodwill." After pointing
out that in the case before him the connection had been formed
by years of work, he went on to say :—" The defendants know
" where to sell the stone, they know where to buy the stone, and
" probably know how to deal to the best advantage in the
" different qualities of the stone. Is it to be supposed that they
" did not sell that personal connection when they sold the trade
" or business and the Goodwill thereof ?"

In *Trego v. Hunt* (1896, A.C. 7), Lord Herschell, after
quoting Sir George Jessel in *Ginesi v. Cooper* (*supra*), said :—
" The present Master of the Rolls took much the same view as
" to what constitutes the Goodwill of a business. I cannot
" myself doubt they were right. It is the connection thus formed,
" together with the circumstances, whether of habit or otherwise,
" which tend to make it permanent that constitutes the Good-
" will of a business. It is this which constitutes the difference
" between a business just started, which has no Goodwill
" attached to it, and one which has acquired a Goodwill. The
" former trader has to seek out his customers from among the
" community as best he can. The latter has a custom ready
" made. He knows what members of the community are pur-

"chasers of the articles in which he deals, and are not attached
"by custom to any other establishment." In the same case Lord
Macnaghten said :—"Generally speaking, it means much more
"than what Lord Eldon took it to mean in *Crutwell v. Lye*
"*(supra)*. . . Often it happens that the Goodwill is the very
"sap and life of the business, without which it would yield little
"or no fruit. It is the whole advantage, whatever it may be, of
"the reputation and connection of the firm, which may have
"been built up by years of honest work, or gained by lavish
"expenditure of money."

In the case of the *Commissioners of Inland Revenue v. Muller,
Lim.* (1901, A.C. 217), which raised a question under the Stamp
Acts, Lord Macnaghten said :—"What is Goodwill? It is a
"thing very easy to describe, very difficult to define. It is the
"benefit and advantage of the good name, reputation, and con-
"nection of a business. It is the attractive force which brings
"in custom. It is the one thing which distinguishes an old-
"established business from a new business at its first start. The
"Goodwill of a business must emanate from a particular centre
"or source. However widely extended or diffused its influence
"may be, Goodwill is worth nothing unless it has power of
"attraction sufficient to bring customers home to the source from
"which it emanates. Goodwill is composed of a variety of
"elements. It differs in its composition in different trades and
"in different businesses in the same trade. One element may
"preponderate here, and another element there."

We may gather from these definitions that where the locality
of the business makes the trade, Goodwill as a disposable asset
represents the advantage derived from the chance that customers
will continue to frequent the premises in which the business has
been carried on ; that where the business is one which depends
upon the reputation of a firm, the Goodwill consists of the
advantage which the owner (whether original or by assignment)
derives from being allowed to represent himself as such ; and

that where the value of the business depends on its business connection, the Goodwill on sale consists of the right to be properly introduced to those connections.

We have so far been considering the Goodwill of a trade. When we come to consider a professional practice—such as a doctor's, or a solicitor's, or such an agency as a stockbroker's, or an Indian commission agent's—more difficult considerations come in. In the earlier cases there was a tendency to treat Goodwill as non-existent in these cases. In *Austen v. Boys* (1858, 27 L.J. Ch. 714), Lord Cranworth said :—" It is very difficult to give " any intelligible meaning to the word ' Goodwill,' as applicable " to the professional practice of a solicitor, in the abstract sense. " When a trade is established in a particular place, the Goodwill " of that trade means nothing more than the sum of money " which any person would be willing to give for the chance of " being able to keep the trade connected with the place where " it has been carried on. It was truly said in argument that " Goodwill is something distinct from the profits of a business, " although, in determining its value, the profits are necessarily " taken into account, and it is usually estimated at so many " years' purchase upon the amount of those profits. But the " term ' Goodwill ' seems wholly inapplicable to the business of " a solicitor, which has no local existence, but is entirely " personal, depending upon the trust and confidence which " persons may repose in his integrity and ability to conduct legal " affairs."

In the case of *Arundel v. Bell* (1883, 52 L.J. Ch. 537), Sir George Jessel took the same view, but Lindley, L.J., refused to lay down any general rule.

In the case of *Steuart v. Gladstone* (1879, 10 Ch.D. 626), Sir George Jessel said he could not understand what the Goodwill of an Indian commission agent could be.

In *May v. Thomson* (1882, 20 Ch.D. 705), the same Judge
dealt with the sale of a medical practice, and said (p. 718) :—
" What is the meaning of selling a medical practice?   It is the
" selling of the introduction of the patients of the doctor who
" sells to the doctor who buys ; he has nothing to sell except the
" introduction.   .   .   .   Therefore when you talk of the sale
" of a non-dispensing medical practice—of course, when a man
" keeps what is called a doctor's shop, there is a different thing
" entirely to sell—you are really talking of the sale of the intro-
" duction to patients, and the length, the character, and the
" duration of the introduction, the terms of the introduction are
" everything."   These difficulties came up for consideration in a
very recent case, *Hill v. Fearis* (1905, 1 Ch. 468).   In this case
Hill and Fearis carried on business as stockbrokers in London
under articles of partnership which contained no mention of
Goodwill.   Hill died, and Fearis continued to carry on the business, and for that purpose obtained the permission of the Committee of the Stock Exchange to use the name of the firm.   He
accounted for Hill's capital, but declined to pay anything in
respect of Goodwill.   His counsel argued that it was not the fact
that every business has a Goodwill, and cited the cases of *Austen
v. Boys* (*supra*) and *Arundel v. Bell* (*supra*) to show that there
was no Goodwill of a solicitor's business.   In this case, too, permission to use the firm name could only be given by the Committee of the Stock Exchange.   To this, counsel for the deceased
partner Hill said :—" Goodwill involves a right to represent that
" you are carrying on the business of the firm, to solicit the
" customers of the old firm, to have the books of the firm, and to
" prevent anybody else from saying that he is carrying on the
" business.   That is quite apart from the right to use the name
" of the firm."   Warrington, J., in giving judgment, quoted the
judgments of Lord Macnaghten and Lord Herschell in *Trego v.
Hunt* (*supra*), and proceeded :—" I summarise this by saying
" the Goodwill of a business is the advantage, whatever it may

" be, which a person gets by continuing to carry on, and being
" entitled to represent to the outside world that he is carrying
" on, a business which has been carried on for some time pre-
" viously. That seems to me to be the meaning of Goodwill.
" . . . It is said that there is no such thing as Goodwill
" in a stockbroker's business, just because of the nature of the
" connection between the stockbroker and those with whom he
" does business. That I do not quite follow. I agree that in
" many cases it may be that the relation between the client and
" the broker is of such a nature that the client would not go with
" his business to the successor in business of the broker; but,
" on the other hand, there are many cases which we can conceive
" in which the client, not knowing who to go to, if he knew that
" his old broker had a successor might well give that man a
" trial, and see whether he would continue to employ him or
" not. I can quite imagine that the successor in business of the
" old broker might, using the expression in *Trego v. Hunt*, get
" an advantage in that way by being able to represent that he
" was carrying on the original business. . . It may not
" be essential to the advantage which I have just pointed out
" . . . . to be able to say that he is using the old name
" or trading under the old name." He accordingly ordered
the Goodwill to be sold, and the proceeds to be accounted for.
The principles here laid down seem applicable to the business of
a solicitor and other similar cases. Wherever there is an
advantage to a person in being able to represent that he is carrying on an old business, there is an asset which has a value of
some sort. Its value will fluctuate with different classes of business, but except in such extreme cases as that of an artist or an
author, whose reputations are absolutely individual to themselves, Goodwill cannot be said to be absolutely non-existent.

It is clear from the extract given above at p. 16 from the judgment in *Kingston Miller & Co. Lim. v. Thos. Kingston & Co.
Lim.* (1912, 1 Ch. 575), that so far as the personal skill of a

servant of an employer contributes to the success of the business, and increases the value of its Goodwill, the advantage of such skill belongs to the employer, and such servant has nothing in the nature of Goodwill, though, of course, he has a personal qualification which he may, on leaving the service of the employer, make use of for his own benefit, or which he may transfer to somebody else. His name is not incident to that qualification in the sense that it can be transferred to a third person.

Goodwill is property, and as such is treated for the purpose of stamp duty on conveyances and on agreements to convey. In *Inland Revenue v. Angus* (1889, 23 Q.B.D. 590), Lord Esher said :—" I have no doubt that the Goodwill of a business is " property within the meaning of the section (there in question). " It is always treated as property between purchaser and seller, " and it is a legal property."

In the case of the *Commissioners of Inland Revenue v. Muller, Lim.* (1901, A.C. 217), an agreement was made in writing to sell the premises of a wholesale manufacturing business carried on abroad, together with the Goodwill of the business, for a lump sum. The vendor covenanted not to engage in any similar trade within fifty miles of the existing premises. All the customers of the business were abroad. The House of Lords held that the Goodwill was " property locally situate out of the United Kingdom" within the meaning of Section 59, Subsection 1, of the Stamp Act, 1891.

Under the Bankruptcy Act, 1883, Section 56, the Goodwill of the bankrupt's business is made property saleable by the trustee. But as to the position of the bankrupt after a sale by his trustee in bankruptcy see *Walker v. Mottram, post.*

In treating Goodwill as property, the law assumes that it is inseparable from a business. Thus in the case of the *Commissioners of Inland Revenue v. Muller, Lim. (supra)*, Lord

Lindley, after giving the definition quoted on p. 2, *supra*, went on to say : " In this wide sense Goodwill is inseparable from " the business to which it adds value, and, in my opinion, exists " where the business is carried on." Again, in the case of *Robertson v. Quiddington* (1860, 28 Beav. 529), a deceased partner had by his will bequeathed the Goodwill of a business to a person who was not a member of the firm. It was held that a testator could not so separate the Goodwill from the business, and that the legacy was invalid. Goodwill may be either real or personal property, according to circumstances. Thus, if it is attached to a freehold house (*e.g.*, a public-house) which is owned by a sole trader, it will be real property. (See *Booth v. Curtis*, 1869, 17 W.R. 393.) And a business has been held to be so linked to the premises where it is carried on that if the premises are compulsorily purchased the business must be paid for as well as the premises. (See *Hunter v. Dowling*, 1895, 2 Ch. 223, and *Commissioners of Inland Revenue v. Muller, Lim.*, *supra*.) But if the premises are the property of a partnership, they are in equity considered as personal property, whether they are freehold or leasehold, as the ultimate object of the partnership is to realise the property and divide the proceeds in money, and equity considers that to be done which is already agreed to be done. Therefore there can be no question but that the Goodwill, or a share in the Goodwill, of a partnership is personal property.

CHAPTER V.

THE ASSIGNMENT OF GOODWILL.

WE have already stated that trade marks and trade names cannot be assigned separately and apart from Goodwill, either by the common law, or in the case of registered trade marks under the provisions of the Trade Marks Act, 1905. The 22nd Section of that Act deals with assignments, and enacts that "a trade mark when registered shall be assigned and trans-"mitted only in connection with the Goodwill of the business "concerned in the goods for which it has been registered, and "shall be determinable with that goodwill. But nothing in this "section contained shall be deemed to affect the right of the "proprietor of a registered trade mark to assign the right to use "the same in any British possession or protectorate or foreign "country in connection with any goods for which it is registered "together with the Goodwill of the business therein in such "goods." In other words, though a trade mark (or a trade name) cannot be sold apart from the business, yet the foreign or colonial trade may be assigned, and with it the right to use the trade mark in such foreign and colonial trade. Goodwill is commonly assigned either (1), on the occasion of a sale of a business; or (2), on the dissolution of a partnership; or (3), on the death of the owner. In the case of a sale of Goodwill no particular formalities need be complied with, and it is not even necessary that the transfer should be recorded in writing (the Statute of Frauds does not apply), nor made in a document under seal. It is hardly necessary to say that it is prudent to have the terms of the sale of a business put into writing.

Goodwill will pass under any words which show an intention to transfer the business. In *Shipwright v. Clements* (1871, 19 W.R. 599) it was decided that the sale of "a business" carried with it the entire Goodwill, though the word was not used in the transaction at all, and that if it carried the Goodwill it passed also the property in a trade mark used in the business, although that also was not specially mentioned.

So in the case of *In re David & Mathews* (1899, 1 Ch. 378) it appeared that the partners in a business had agreed in the partnership articles that "in case of the death of one of the "partners a general account of the position shall be made, "including all effects and securities of whatsoever nature that "they possess, and the value of such effects and securities be "estimated as at the date of such decease." It was held that the arbitrator ought to consider the Goodwill as included under "effects and securities of whatsoever nature." See also the case of *Jennings v. Jennings* (1898, 1 Ch., p. 378), *infra*, p. 58, where Goodwill was held to pass under the words "assets of the business." On the sale of a business to a company which is about to issue a prospectus inviting the public to subscribe for shares or debentures, attention must be paid to the requirements of the Companies (Consolidation) Act, 1908, under Section 81 (1) (g) of which, in stating the amounts paid or payable as purchase-money in cash, shares, or debentures for any property purchased or acquired by the company, or proposed so to be, the amount payable for Goodwill must be separately specified.

We shall deal in a separate chapter with questions of Goodwill arising on a dissolution of partnership, and it is not necessary to say more than a word here on acquisition by death of the owner. The Goodwill of a business may be bequeathed or devised by a testator so long as he does not try to separate it from the business. (See *Robertson v. Quiddington, supra* p. 51.)

If the deceased has died intestate the Goodwill will pass to the next-of-kin, or his heir-at-law, according as it happens to be personal or real property, as to which see Chapter IV., *supra.*

The next question to consider is, What rights does the assignee of the Goodwill of a business obtain?

The main rights of the assignee of the Goodwill are the right to represent that he is carrying on the business of the firm, to prevent anybody else from saying that he is carrying on the business, to solicit the customers of the old firm, to have the books of the firm, and to use the trade marks, if there are any. Besides this, the assignee *may* have the right to prevent the former owner from soliciting the old customers, and *may* have the right to use the name of the firm. The rights that invariably pass to the assignee present no difficulty, and have been sufficiently explained already. The questions as to the right of the former owner to compete with the assignee, and of the right of the assignee to use the trade name, require more detailed examination.

COMPETITION BY FORMER OWNER.—The law as to the rights of the vendor of the Goodwill of a business after the sale by him of the Goodwill was for a long time a matter of doubt, but has been recently laid down with precision in the case of *Trego v. Hunt* (1896, A.C. 7). That case restored the authority of the earlier case of *Labouchere v. Dawson* (1872, 13 Eq. 322), where it was decided that neither by agent, by letter, nor privately must the vendor of the Goodwill solicit the custom of those who were habitual dealers with the firm, the Goodwill of which has been sold. In *Trego v. Hunt* the respondent to the appeal was in partnership with the appellant, and one of the terms of the partnership was that the appellant should be the sole owner of the Goodwill of the business after the termination of the partnership. Not long before that period arrived the respondent caused a list of the names of the customers of the firm to be made out, and his avowed object in so doing was to make it easy for him thereafter to canvass them on his own account. The appellant applied for an injunction to stop this, a relief to which for the moment he was not strictly entitled, as the partnership had not actually come to an end. But to bring the matter to a head the parties agreed that the Court should give its decision upon the assumption that the firm had been dissolved, that the Goodwill belonged to the appellant, and that the respondent was soliciting the customers of the firm in competition with the appellant, the assignee of the Goodwill. The ultimate decision is thus stated in the head-note to the report in the Law Reports :—" Where the Goodwill of a business is sold " (without further provision), the vendor may set up a rival " business, but he is not entitled to canvass the customers of " the old firm, and may be restrained by injunction from " soliciting any person who was a customer of the old firm prior " to the sale to continue to deal with the vendor, or not to deal " with the purchaser. The same principle is applicable to the " case where a person has been taken into partnership on the " terms that on the expiration of the partnership the Goodwill " of the business shall belong solely to the other partner."

Lord Herschell said :—" I think it must be treated as settled " that whenever the Goodwill of a business is sold the vendor " does not, by reason only of that scale, come under a restriction " not to carry on a competing business. . . . It does not " seem to me to follow that because a man may, by his acts, " invite all men to deal with him, and so amongst the rest of " mankind, invite the former customers of the firm, he may use " the knowledge which he has acquired of what persons were " customers of the old firm, in order, by an appeal to them, to " seek to weaken their habit of dealing where they have dealt " before, or whatever else binds them to the old business, and so

" to secure their custom for himself.   This seems to me a direct
" and intentional dealing with the Goodwill, and an endeavour
" to destroy it.   If a person who has previously been a partner
" in the firm sets up in business on his own account, and appeals
" generally for custom, he only does that which any member of
" the public may do, and which those carrying on the same trade
" are already doing.   It is true that those who were former
" customers of the firm to which he belonged may of their own
" accord transfer their custom to him ; but this incidental
" advantage is unavoidable, and does not result from any act of
" his.   He only conducts his business in precisely the same way
" as he would if he had never been a member of the firm to
" which he previously belonged.   But when he specifically and
" directly appeals to those who were customers of the previous
" firm he seeks to take advantage of the connection previously
" formed by his old firm, and of the knowledge of that connec-
" tion which he has previously acquired, to take that which
" constitutes the Goodwill away from the persons to whom it has
" been sold, and to restore it to himself."

Lord Macnaghten said :—" And so it has resulted that a
" person who sells the Goodwill of his business is under no
" obligation to retire from the field.   Trade he undoubtedly may,
" and in the very same line of business.   If he has not bound
" himself by special stipulation, and if there is no evidence of
" the understanding of the parties beyond that which is to be
" found in all cases, he is free to carry on business wherever he
" chooses.   But, then, how far may he go?   He may do every-
" thing that a stranger to the business, in ordinary course,
" would be in a position to do. - He may set up where he will.
" He may push his wares as much as he pleases.   He may thus
" interfere with the custom of his neighbour as a stranger and
" outsider might do ; but he must not, I think, avail himself of
" his special knowledge of the old customers to regain, without
" consideration, that which he has parted with for value.   He

" must not make his approaches from the vantage ground of his
" former position, moving under cover of a connection which is
" no longer his. He may not sell the custom and steal away the
" customers in that fashion. . . . It is quite true that it
" would be better that the purchaser should protect himself by
" taking apt covenants from the person with whom he is deal-
" ing. But this, I think, is rather a counsel of perfection than a
" reason for leaving the purchaser entirely at the mercy of the
" vendor."

It will be seen from Lord Macnaghten's judgment that a purchaser who desires to be absolutely safe from lawful competition on the part of the vendor should obtain from the vendor
a promise binding him not to compete within such limits of time
and space as may reasonably be necessary to give effect to the
purchase. Such an agreement will not be void as being in
restraint of trade, provided that it is not wider than is necessary
for the protection of the purchaser. (*Nordenfeldt v. Maxim-
Nordenfeldt*, 1894, A.C. 535.) On a subsequent sale of the
Goodwill the benefit of such a promise will pass with the Goodwill. (*Townsend v. Jarman*, 1900, 2 Ch. 698.) In the case of
Curl Brothers, Lim. v. Webster (1904, 1 Ch. 685), a novel point
was raised. The vendor of the Goodwill set up a rival business,
and some of his old customers, without solicitation, came to
trade with him. Could he solicit these customers to continue to
trade with him? It was held that the rule laid down in *Trego
v. Hunt* ought not to be limited so as to exclude persons who
before solicitation have of their own accord become customers
of the vendor in his rival business.

The rule laid down in *Trego v. Hunt* only applies where the
vendor of the Goodwill is the person who has himself carried on
the business. But it may happen that the person who has carried
on the business has become bankrupt, and the Goodwill is sold
not by himself, but by the trustee in his bankruptcy. It was
held in the case of *Walker v. Mottram* (1881, 19 Ch.D. 355) that

a bankrupt whose business has been sold by the trustee in the bankruptcy could not be restrained from setting up *bonâ fide* a fresh business, and soliciting the customers of the former business. The considerations which apply in this and other cases where the vendor is not the person who has carried on the business were discussed in the case of *Jennings v. Jennings* (1898, 1 Ch. 378). In this case A. and B. had formerly carried on business in partnership, and B. had brought an action for rescission of the partnership, on the ground of misrepresentations of A. This action was compromised on the terms that judgment should be entered for B. for £1,200, the partnership to be dissolved, A. retaining the assets. The Goodwill was not specifically mentioned in the terms of the compromise. A. subsequently brought another action to restrain B. from canvassing the customers of the old firm. The line taken in argument was that B. was not in the position of a vendor, and that the sale had really been made by the Court, and that the rule laid down in *Walker v. Mottram* should be applied, and not the rule laid down in *Trego v. Hunt.*

Mr. Justice Stirling decided that the relation of vendor and purchaser existed between the parties, that B. was subject to the ordinary obligations of a vendor, and that consequently upon the authority of *Trego v. Hunt* A. was entitled to an injunction. The following passage from his judgment deserves careful attention :—" The obligation to refrain from canvassing " customers arises out of the relation of vendor and purchaser. " Thus Lord Macnaghten says (in *Trego v. Hunt*), ' The prin- " ' ciple on which *Labouchere v. Dawson* (*supra*) rests has been " ' presented in various ways. A man may not derogate from his " ' own grant; the vendor is not at liberty to destroy or " ' depreciate the thing which he has sold ; there is an implied " ' covenant on the sale of Goodwill that the vendor does not " ' solicit the custom which he has parted with ; it would be a " ' fraud on the contract to do so. These, as it seems to me, are " ' only different turns and glimpses of a proposition which I

" ' take to be elementary. It is not right to profess and to
" ' purport to sell that which you do not mean the purchaser to
" ' have ; it is not an honest thing to pocket the price, and then
" ' to recapture the subject of sale, to decoy it away, or call it
" ' back before the purchaser has had time to attach it to himself,
" ' and make it his very own.' . . . The source of the
" obligation is well shown by the decision in *Walker v.*
" *Mottram*, where it was held that a bankrupt, the Goodwill
" of whose business had been sold by the trustee in bankruptcy,
" could not be restrained from setting up *bonâ fide* a fresh
" business, and soliciting the customers of his former business,
" not because the Goodwill of a business sold by a trustee in
" bankruptcy differs from that sold by a solvent man, but
" simply because the bankrupt is not the vendor, and conse-
" quently is under no liability towards the purchaser. That
" that was the ground of the decision . . . is pointed
" out by Lord Macnaghten in *Trego v Hunt*, where he expresses
" approval of the decision, saying :—' There is all the difference
" ' in the world between the case of a man who sells what belongs
" ' to himself and receives the consideration, and a man whose
" ' property is sold without his consent by his trustee in bank-
" ' ruptcy, and who comes under no obligation, express or
" ' implied, to the purchaser from the trustee.' "

In the case of *Green & Sons (Northampton) Lim. v. Morris*
(1914, 1 Ch. 562) it was held that the general principle of
Trego v. Hunt does not apply to a case of a sale of a debtor's
business by the trustee of a Deed of Arrangement executed by
the debtor for the benefit of his creditors. In such a case the
alienation being involuntary, as in the case of bankruptcy,
the exception established in *Walker v. Mottram* applies, and the
debtor is not precluded from soliciting the customers of the
firm.

RIGHT TO THE USE OF THE TRADE NAME.—Frequently the
most valuable of the rights which should pass to the man who

acquires a business is the right to trade in the name under which
the business has acquired its reputation.   But the name cannot
always pass.   For instance, in the case of *Hill v. Fearis* (1905,
1 Ch. 466) we saw that the right to decide who might use the
partnership name of a firm of stockbrokers rested with the Stock
Exchange Committee.   In the case of solicitors, where the business name is that of a living solicitor it would probably be a
hazardous matter for the purchaser of the business to practise
under that name.   But these are exceptional cases.   The
authorities on the general question have recently been reviewed
in the Court of Appeal in the case of *Burchell v. Wilde* (1900,
1 Ch. 551).   The Court there accepted the following passage
from the judgment in *Thynne v. Shove* (1890, 45 Ch.D. 577) as a
clear statement of the result of the authorities.   " He, the plain-
" tiff, has assigned the Goodwill of his business to the defen-
" dant; and by virtue of that assignment the defendant, in
" carrying on the business, has the right to use the name of
" the assignor for the purpose of showing that the business
" is the business formerly carried on by the assignor; and he
" has the full right so to use it, subject to this : that he must
" not exercise that right so as to expose the assignor to any
" liability by holding him out to be the real owner of the busi
" ness.   That is the only limit of the defendant's right to use
" the plaintiff's name."

Whether there will be any risk of exposing the assignor to
liability will depend upon the circumstances of each case.

In the case of *Scott v. Rowland* (1872, 26 L.T. 391) there was
a discussion on some of the earlier cases.   This was a case
where, on the dissolution of partnership, the whole of the stock-
in-trade was purchased at a valuation by one of the partners, but
no assignment was made of the Goodwill of the business.   The
Vice-Chancellor said :—" Even assuming that the Goodwill had
" been effectually assigned to the defendant, it would still be a
" question whether he would have a right to use the plaintiff's

"name. The law as laid down in *Churton v. Douglas* (1859, 28
"L.J. Ch. 841) makes an outgoing partner, who leaves his
"name in the style of the firm, liable to some extent for the
"debts of the firm. For instance, he would be *primâ facie*
"liable on bills of exchange. In *Banks v. Gibson* (1865, 34
"Beav. 566) the outgoing partner was dead, and the case only
"goes to show that, as no liability can attach to an outgoing
"partner who is dead or bankrupt, there is no reason why his
"name should not be retained, but it is different where he is
"living. The injunction must be granted restraining the
"defendant 'from using the plaintiff's name in connection with
"'his business as a glass stainer, so as to represent that the
"'plaintiff is a partner in the business.'"

In the case of *Levy v. Walker* (1879, 10 Ch.D. 436) two
partners, Charbonnel and Walker, carried on business as
"Charbonnel & Walker," in London. Charbonnel, who was
an unmarried lady, married Levy, and the business partnership with Charbonnel was dissolved on the terms that the
partnership business, Goodwill, &c., should be sold as a going
concern to the highest bidder of the two partners. Walker
bought the business; Mr. and Mrs. Levy then lived in Paris.
The business was thereafter carried on in London under the
old style, "Charbonnel & Walker." Of this Mrs. Levy com-
plained, and unsuccessfully asked the Court to restrain Walker
from trading under that name. Sir George Jessel said that,
on the sale of the Goodwill, "the name is part of the assets."
In the course of his judgment James, L.J., said :—"But there
"is another point upon which I myself cannot entertain any
"doubt, which is this, that the assignment of the Goodwill and
"business of Charbonnel & Walker did convey the right to use
"the name of Charbonnel & Walker, and the exclusive right to
"use that name as between the vendor and the purchaser of
"that business. . . . I think it right to say that the sale
"of the Goodwill and business conveyed the right to the use of

"" the partnership name as a description of the articles sold in
"" the trade, and that the right is an exclusive right as against
"" the person who sold it, and an exclusive right as against all the
"" world, so that no other person could represent himself as carry-
"" ing on the same business." The Court of Appeal, in
Burchell v. Wilde (see p. 60 *supra*), recognised *Levy v.
Walker* as a sound decision on the circumstances there
disclosed, because there was obviously no risk that the use
of the name Charbonnel in London would expose Mrs. Levy,
living in Paris, to any liability, even though her name had been
Charbonnel before her marriage. The Court held that " it is
"" not to be read as determining that the purchaser of a business
"" and Goodwill is entitled to use the style of the old firm,
"" if that style includes the name of a living person, or if the use
"" of it would expose the owner of such name to liability." In
the case of *Thynne v. Shove*, *supra* p. 60, Thynne had sold his
baker's business to Shove, the Goodwill being expressly assigned,
as also was the stock-in-trade. Amongst the stock and utensils
were paper bags and business cards, with Thynne's name upon
them. Thynne desired to restrain Shove from using the cards
and from trading in the name of Thynne. The decision arrived
at was that Shove might use the name of Thynne for the purpose
of showing that the business he now carried on was that formerly
carried on by Thynne, but that he must exercise that right in
such manner as not to render Thynne liable to the creditors of
that business.

The facts in *Burchell v. Wilde* were as follow :—In 1882 a
partnership of solicitors was constituted, the partners being
W. Burchell the elder, W. Burchell the younger, the defendant
W. G. Wilde, and the plaintiffs J. W. Burchell and C. T. D.
Burchell, and they carried on business under the style of
Burchell & Co. In June 1893, W. Burchell the elder having
died, and W. Burchell the younger having retired, the plaintiffs
and the defendant agreed to continue in partnership under the

same style of Burchell & Co. In the year 1899 the partnership was dissolved by consent, there being no sale of the Goodwill and assets, and no provision as to the use of the firm-name. Both the plaintiffs and the defendant (with a partner) proceeded to carry on business as Burchell & Co., but at separate offices. The plaintiffs claimed the exclusive right to use the name Burchell, or Burchells, and to restrain the defendants from using either of those names in any way as part of their firm-name. It was held by Byrne, J., that the right to an injunction depended upon the plaintiffs establishing that any use of the word " Burchell " as part of the name of the defendant's firm would expose the plaintiffs to risk of liability, and the Court, not being satisfied that either of the plaintiffs would be under any tangible risk of liability if the defendants were to practise as Burchell, Wilde & Co. (as they said they were willing to do), especially if the plaintiffs were to use a style carrying their initials, made no order.

The Court of Appeal held that, subject to the above limitation as to exposing the plaintiffs to liability, the defendants were entitled to use the name Burchell & Co., though it would be more satisfactory to alter their name in the way they had undertaken to do.

It will be noticed in this case that " Burchell & Co." was not the name of a living person, but was itself a fancy name, though suggesting that the partners had the family name of Burchell.

CHAPTER VI.

PARTNERSHIP AND GOODWILL.

THE Goodwill is, in the absence of express agreement, the common property of the members of the partnership; they are each and all entitled to their share of the benefits to be derived from it. Hence, when the firm is dissolved, it is the right of each of the partners to have the Goodwill sold for the benefit of all, and this is the same whether the dissolution arises on the death of a partner or otherwise. " Up to comparatively recent times it " was considered that the right to the Goodwill belonged to the " surviving partners, and it is only recently that the importance " of Goodwill and the necessity of preventing its improper " appropriation have been fully recognised." (*In re David & Mathews*, 1899, 1 Ch. 378.) The latest decision on this point is the case of *Hill v. Fearis* (1905, 1 Ch. 466). The head-note in that case is as follows :—" Hill & Fearis carried on business " as stockbrokers in London, under articles of partnership which " contained no mention of Goodwill. Hill died and Fearis con- " tinued to carry on the business. For this purpose he obtained " the permission of the Committee of the Stock Exchange to use " the name of the firm. He accounted for Hill's capital, but " declined to pay anything in respect of Goodwill : Held, that " the nature of a stockbroker's business was not such that there " could not be a saleable Goodwill thereof, and that, *in the* " *absence of any provisions to the contrary in the articles*, the " Goodwill must be sold and the proceeds accounted for." This right of sale is not as valuable as it appears on the surface, as the surviving partners may compete with the purchaser of the Goodwill, and thus reduce its value considerably, if not to nothing. The case of *Wilson v. Williams* (1892, 29 L.R. Ir. 176) has been quoted as an authority for the Court refusing a sale of the Goodwill on this ground; but Mr. Justice Warrington, in the case of *Hill v. Fearis*, just quoted, refused to accept it as an authority for such a course, as it was decided before *Trego v. Hunt*, and was probably based on a misconception of the law as to the solicitation of old customers.

This question of competition is an important factor, and has long been so recognised. The order made in the old case of *Cook v. Collingridge* (1825, 27 Beav. 456), in the winding-up of a partnership which had expired by effluxion of time, was as follows :—" And the Court doth declare that no Court can " prevent the late partners from engaging in the same business, " and therefore that the sale cannot proceed upon the same " principle as if a Court could prevent them so engaging, and " doth declare that in this case, as it appears to this Court to be " circumstanced, the valuation and estimate is and can only be " that which every bidder according to his own speculations can " fancy to be the worth of his chance of retaining old customers, " and their not following the old partners, or any of them, into " a new establishment, and doth declare that it seems to this " Court also, in the circumstances of the case, to be advisable " to allow the old partners, or any of them, or any persons " interested, to bid for or propose to be buyers of the concern." In *Hall v. Barrows* (1863, 4 De Gex. J. & S., 151) the facts were as follows :—By the articles of partnership it was in effect provided that in case either of the parties should die during the partnership the surviving partner should have the option of taking to himself all the stock belonging to the partnership, or paying its value. The Court below had held that it was clear that the word " stock " included all which the articles declared

should constitute the capital of the partnership—viz., " the iron-
" works, &c., and the stock-in-trade, implements, tools, and other
" property belonging to the business "—and the only controversy
was as to its including the Goodwill and a trade mark.   The
defendant had agreed to buy at a valuation whatever the Court
decided to be included in the word " stock." After deciding that
the trade mark was included, Lord Westbury's judgment proceeded :—" The remaining question relates to the Goodwill of
" the business.   I agree with the Master of the Rolls that Good-
" will ought to be included in any sale or valuation as a distinct
" subject of value, but I think it necessary that the direction to
" value the Goodwill should be accompanied by a declaration
" defining what is meant by it, at least negatively—that is to say,
" a declaration that the Goodwill is not to be valued upon the
" principle that the surviving partner, if he were not the pur-
" chaser, will be restrained from setting up the same description
" of business.   No such restriction could be thrown on the
" surviving partner if the sale were to a stranger ; but still, even
" without any such restriction, there may be a subject of value
" directed by the term ' Goodwill ' that ought to be taken into
" account in making the valuation."

In the case of *In re David & Mathews* (1899, 1 Ch. 378) the
agreement in the partnership articles was that, " in case of the
" death of one of the partners a general account of the position
" shall be made, including all effects and securities of whatso-
" ever nature that they possess, and the value of such effects and
" securities be estimated as at the date of such decease."   It was
held " that the arbitrator ought to consider the question of
" Goodwill (if any), and to set such a value upon it as he
" might consider to have been attached at the death of D. (the
" deceased partner), and that the value (if any) of the Goodwill
" ought to be appraised on the footing that, if it were sold, the
" surviving partner would be at liberty to carry on a rival busi-
" ness, but would not have the right to solicit any person who

" was a customer of the old firm prior to the death of D., or the
" right to carry on business under the name of L. & D. (the style
" of the old firm)." This decision followed the lines laid down
in *Trego v. Hunt* (1896, A.C. 7), the head-note to which has
already been given on p. 55.

It is a matter of prudence in drawing partnership articles to
see that express provisions are inserted as to the Goodwill.

It should be noted that the Courts, in dealing with these cases
of Partnership and Goodwill, seem to recognise a difference
between the annual accounts of the partners and the final
account made on dissolution. And it does not follow that
because the value of the Goodwill does not appear in the annual
accounts, that it is therefore not to be included in the final
account. In *Barrow v. Barrow* (1872, 27 L.T.N.S. 431) the outgoer was entitled to a share, according to valuation, of all
" effects and things " belonging to the partnership; and the
Court decided that, under these words, he acquired a right to
have the Goodwill taken into account, though, whilst a member
of the firm, he had habitually signed accounts in which nothing
was put down for Goodwill. In *Wade v. Jenkins* (1860, 2 Giff.
509) the partnership articles valued the Goodwill at £6,000,
but provided that it should not be taken into the partnership
accounts. Further, it was provided that, on the determination
of the partnership, a general account should be taken. The
Court decided that on the retirement of a partner the retiring
partner was entitled to have an allowance for his share of the
Goodwill. Where, however, the annual account, in which
Goodwill is not taken into account, is expressly made the basis
of the final account, Goodwill is necessarily excluded from that
account as well. In the case of *Steuart v. Gladstone* (1879,
10 Ch.D. 626), the partnership articles provided that each year a
general account should be taken of the " stocks, moneys, debts,
&c., . . . and other estate and effects," and a fair valuation of everything " susceptible of valuation " should be made

up to the 30th April for the purposes of getting at profit and loss ; on retirement of a partner the last valuation *for ascertaining profits and losses* was to be the basis of paying out. The Court of Appeal held that there could be nothing allowed to an outgoer for his share of the Goodwill, basing its decision upon the words in italics, and upon the fact that the business was of such a nature that there could hardly be any Goodwill connected with it.

In *Hunter v. Dowling* (1895, 2 Ch. 223) the articles of partnership provided that if any partner should die during the continuance of the partnership, the amount of his share and interest should be taken at the amount appearing as standing to his credit at the last annual Balance Sheet which should have been signed previously to his death. These annual Balance Sheets did not include Goodwill. A partner died on 10th April 1891, at a time when a railway company intended to acquire the premises of the firm, and had served its notice to treat. and the firm was on the point of realising a very handsome sum for the premises and business. The Court held that the deceased partner must stand by the account of the preceding 31st March. " Any of the partners might have died, and if any of them had " died it is clear that, under the articles, the value of the Good- " will, not being included in the last Balance Sheet, his estate " would not be paid for it."

Smith v. Nelson (1904, 92 L.T. 313) is another quite recent case where, on the construction of the partnership articles, it was decided that the outgoing partner was not entitled to anything for Goodwill.

The question of the use of the partnership name after dissolution is also one of great practical importance. If the Goodwill is sold the purchaser has a right to hold himself out as the successor of the partnership in the business, and none of the old partners may carry on business in the old name. It sometimes happens, however, that where the Goodwill is not of

especial value, as in the case of a solicitor's business, a dissolution of partnership takes place without any sale or assignment
of the Goodwill of the business, and without any provision as
to the use of the firm name.   In such a case the rule was laid
down in *Burchell v. Wilde* (1900, 1 Ch. 551) that each of the
partners is entitled to carry on business under that name, provided
that he does not by so doing expose his former partners to any
risk of liability.   Whether there will be any such risk is a matter
to be determined, having regard to the circumstances of each
case.   In the Court of Appeal it was said :—" It was left
" entirely undecided what was to be done about the use of the
" name of the firm.   But if you come to the conclusion (about
" which there can be no doubt) that the Goodwill apart from
" the benefit of the firm-name, as to which nothing is said, was
" not to be sold, but was to be divided between the partners, what
" is the result ?   It appears to me to follow that each partner
" could use the name of the old firm.   They had become tenants-
" in-common of that asset, and each partner was entitled to
" enjoy that asset, subject only to a limitation as to his not
" exposing his former partners to any risk of liability."   In the
case of *Townsend v. Jarman* (1900, 2 Ch. 698) it was similarly
laid down that, unless the right to use the firm-name is expressly
assigned, the assignee of the Goodwill must not use the name
so as to expose any partner to liability.   In this case the firm-
name was Jarman & Co., and the partner's name Jarman.   The
Court held that Jarman could not complain of the use of the
name " Jarman & Co."   " The defendant's name is not, and
" never has been, Jarman & Co., and a man is not held out as
" a partner by the use of a name which is not his own."

CHAPTER VII.

GOODWILL AND ACCOUNTS.

THE law has not much to say as to the keeping of accounts, and, except where legal principles are directly involved, leaves accountants to manage their own business in their own way. In the case of a sole trader, it matters little whether Goodwill does or does not appear in his accounts. The business is his, and no bookkeeping entries can increase or diminish its value, or bring his claims into conflict with the claims of others. There is only one case which we need notice. There is a provision in Section 47 of the Bankruptcy Act to the effect that a settlement of more than two years' standing, and less than ten years' standing, is void on the subsequent bankruptcy of the settlor, unless the settlor can show that at the time he settled his property he was able to pay his debts, irrespective of the property settled. In *Ex parte Russell* (1882, 19 Ch.D. 588) the question was raised whether the Goodwill of the settlor's business could be taken into account. Sir George Jessel said :—" It is suggested, " however, that the Goodwill of the baker's business was worth " something. I dare say it was, but can that be called an avail· " able asset when a man is carrying on his trade? Is he able to " pay all his debts because he might possibly, after the lapse of " a considerable time, sell the Goodwill of the business? The " debts were presently payable. How can a man be said to be " able to pay his debts because he has a business the Goodwill " of which he may be able to sell? It is quite plain that this is " not an asset which ought to be reckoned within the purview " of this section."

When we come to partnership we have already seen that in some cases the final account between partners, on which an outgoing or deceased partner is paid his share, may be based on an annual account which does not include Goodwill.

We may take it that Goodwill should not be included in annual Partnership Accounts.

In *Smith v. Nelson* (1904, 92 L.T. 313) Mr. Justice Joyce said :—" The annual accounts directed by Clause 7 had " regularly been taken, as such accounts usually are, without any " regard to the value, whatever it was, of the Goodwill. The " Goodwill never had been, and never was, brought into the " annual or any other account of the partnership. It was not " contended before me, nor in my opinion, having regard to the " well-known case of *Steuart v. Gladstone*, could it have been " contended with any prospect of success that the value of the " Goodwill ought to have been included in any of the annual " accounts."

The following are the passages in the judgments in *Steuart v. Gladstone* (1879, 10 Ch.D. 626) which relate to the making out of the annual accounts. The clause in the particular articles of partnership dealt with in this case said that the annual accounts were to comprise " all particulars that might be susceptible of valuation." Sir George Jessel said :—" Then is " it a fair construction of these articles to assume that, in taking " the annual accounts of the profits of the concern, the partners " were going to put a value upon the Goodwill, so as to allow " each partner to take year by year out of the partnership the " amount of his share of the increase in the value of the Good- " will ? That is really what it comes to. Now one cannot help " feeling that no mercantile man ever dreamt of such a thing. " The Goodwill is not an available asset in the sense that you " can draw upon it, or that you can turn it into money, or pay it " out to the partners, and I should say with some confidence, not " only relying upon my own experience, but having appealed to

" the Bar in this case, that no one ever saw such a thing in a
" merchant's accounts."

James, L. J., said :—" Is it reasonable, and could anyone ever
" suppose that a changing thing like Goodwill, the value of
" which would vary year by year according to the state of trade
" in the countries in which this firm was carrying on its business,
" and according to the reputation which the house had acquired,
" or had lost, for integrity, punctuality, solvency, and mercantile
" prudence, was to be valued from year to year, and that the
" partners were to say, 'Our Goodwill last year was worth
" ' £10,000, this year it is only worth £9,000, then carry the
" ' £1,000 to Profit and Loss,' or 'Last year our Goodwill was
" ' only worth £10,000, this year it is worth £15,000, carry the
" ' £5,000 to profit.' That seems to be somewhat a *reductio ad
" absurdum* with reference to bringing it into the accounts under
" this article."

But though Goodwill is not properly brought into the annual
accounts of a partnership, yet if there is nothing expressly to
the contrary in the articles of partnership, or the annual
accounts are not made the basis of the final account, Goodwill
must be brought in when this final account is made up. See the
cases of *Barrow v. Barrow* and *Wade v. Jenkins* on p. 53.

As to the accounts of companies, we have already seen that a
company which issues a prospectus inviting subscriptions for
shares or debentures must state the amount of purchase-money
which is being paid for Goodwill. This amount will therefore
naturally appear as a separate item in the Capital Account. As
regards annual accounts, the principles laid down in *Steuart v.
Gladstone* seem to apply equally well to both partnerships and
companies. But any special account of the nature of a complete
account of the assets should contain a fair estimate of the value
of the Goodwill. Both these propositions receive support from
the following passage in the judgment in *Barrow Hæmatite Steel
Co.* (1900, 2 Ch. 846), in which an application was made to the

Court for leave to reduce capital, on the ground that part of the capital had been lost, or was unrepresented by available assets. " As to Goodwill, it is no doubt true that the company never has " entered Goodwill as an asset. For the purposes of the com- " pany as a going concern there was no necessity for doing this ; " but, nevertheless, any Goodwill must be regarded as an avail- " able asset for the purpose of a reduction petition. . . . I " think upon the balance of the evidence that a company of this " magnitude, whose goods are known all over the world by their " particular brand, must have a Goodwill of considerable value."

This judgment also quoted the decision of Mr. Justice North, in the case of *In re Abstainers' and General Insurance Co.* (1891, 2 Ch. 124). Here there was a deficiency of £8,555 on the Insurance Fund. £15,452 had been sunk on preliminary expenses, agency establishment, and extension expenses. Mr. Justice North said, during the argument, " If the company " were transferring its business to another company, the Good- " will would probably be an available asset of some value " ; and remarked, in his judgment, " I cannot take it simply on the " statement contained in the petition that the capital which was " expended on preliminary expenses is now unrepresented by " available assets."

CHAPTER VIII.

THE VALUATION OF GOODWILL.

Many circumstances have to be taken into consideration before the value of the Goodwill of any particular undertaking can be arrived at, and, further, the circumstances that are of importance in one case are by no means invariably the same as those that require to be considered in another. There are, however, certain fundamental conditions which must always exist before it can properly be said that Goodwill is of any appreciable value, and they are that the person to whom the Goodwill passes must in all cases have

(1) The right to carry on business at the same place as that at which it was formerly carried on ;

(2) The right to use the old name, and to represent himself as the legitimate successor of the former proprietors ;

(3) The exclusive right to so represent himself (which involves an agreement between the former proprietors and their successor not to compete in the same class of business within a reasonable distance of his place of business and for a reasonable time, it being understood that the term '' reasonable '' in this connection must be construed after taking into consideration the precise nature of each particular class of undertaking).

(4) The full control of the books of the business. including all lists of the names and addresses of customers, &c.

Before going further into this question of the valuation of Goodwill, it seems desirable to point out the various circumstances under which such a valuation may become necessary, They are as follow :—

(1) The sale of the whole undertaking by a retiring proprietor or proprietors ;

(2) The sale of the whole undertaking by the executors of a deceased proprietor or proprietors ;

(3) The sale of a share in the undertaking by an existing proprietor to an incoming partner ;

(4) The sale of a retiring partner's share in the undertaking to an incoming partner ;

(5) The sale of a deceased partner's share in the undertaking to an incoming partner ;

(6) The sale of an expelled partner's share in the undertaking to an incoming partner ;

(7) The sale of a retiring (or deceased) partner's share in the undertaking to the continuing partners ;

(8) The sale of an expelled partner's share of the undertaking to the continuing partners.

The considerations which have to be borne in mind under these various circumstances are as follow :—

(1) Will the retiring proprietor, or proprietors, *assist* the new undertaking so far as lies in his (or their) power?

(2) Will they *oppose* the new undertaking so far as lies in their power?

(3) Is it *beyond their power* to either assist or oppose the new undertaking?

These latter are points which are, perhaps, too little considered in arriving at a valuation of Goodwill; but in the vast majority of instances they form, perhaps, the most powerful factor in connection with arriving at a proper basis of value.

For instance, if one of several partners dies, under all ordinary circumstances the Goodwill of the undertaking (in so far as it has any real value) would naturally be acquired by the continuing partners, whether or not they actually purchased it from the executors of the deceased partner; and it is only on grounds of equity that they could be asked to pay anything for the deceased partner's share of the Goodwill, inasmuch as, for all practical purposes, it would devolve upon them *ipso facto*. But for this very reason—that they *do* absolutely get the full value of the deceased partner's share—it may be said that, if it is proper that they should pay anything at all, it is proper that they should pay a higher value than might be assessed under other circumstances; and, as a matter of fact, most partnership deeds provide that, in the event of the death of one partner during the continuance of the term, the amount to be paid to his executors by the continuing partners shall be something which is at least up to the full marketable value of the deceased partner's share in the Goodwill of the business.   Probably the prevalence of this custom is due to a desire on the part of all partners to make some provision for their family in the case of death; but, in addition to this natural desire upon the part of every person contemplating a partnership, there is, on the other hand, the equally natural feeling that, in the event of his partner dying, the continuing partner will, no doubt, derive a far greater benefit from the business than if a dissolution by consent had been arranged during the continuance of the contemplated term, under which one partner was to pay out the other.

Provision for this event by means of an insurance policy on the joint lives of the partners is becoming daily more common, and it might be possible to arrange such a matter so as to obviate any difficulties with regard to Goodwill, but the movement is yet in its infancy, and therefore perhaps little is to be gained by discussing academic possibilities.   It may be pointed out, however, that the correct method of charging up insurance premiums under such circumstances is *not* to charge them generally against the profits of the firm, nor yet to charge each partner with the cost of insuring his own life : the equitable plan is rather to charge each partner with his due proportion (having regard to his share of profits) of the cost of insuring the lives of each of his co-partners. Thus if A., B., and C. divide profits in the proportions of one-half, one-third, and one-sixth (*i.e.*, in the ratios of 3, 2, 1), then two-thirds of the cost of insuring A.'s life should be borne by B., and one-third by C. ; three-fourths of the cost of insuring B.'s life should be borne by A.. and one-fourth by C. ; and three-fifths of the cost of insuring C.'s life should be borne by A. and two-fifths by B.

Coming next to the case of a person acquiring the Goodwill of a business from a person who proposes to retire therefrom, it will be obvious that the principal question which the purchaser will ask himself is as to how far, if at all, he will really step into the shoes of the vendor ; and it is according to the probabilities of his actually so doing that he will be prepared to pay more or less for the Goodwill that is supposed to be conveyed to him. Thus, if a sole trader sells a portion of his business to an incoming partner—or if a purchaser acquires the share of a partner who is retiring without any intention of setting up in business elsewhere—that purchaser will naturally be disposed to pay a considerably higher amount for the Goodwill that he acquires than he would be inclined to pay—were he to acquire the whole of the business from a retiring proprietor, or the share of a business that had formerly been owned by a partner who had been expelled, or who (having retired) contemplated carrying on business elsewhere. Under the first set of circumstances this would be so because the purchaser would not only be placed nominally in the position of the vendor, but would also have the benefit of such *introductions* as the vendor is able to afford him, together with the whole weight of his

personal influence, which undoubtedly is in many businesses of
the greatest possible value.   On the other hand, supposing one
of three partners is expelled by the others, and the continuing
two take in a new third partner, the latter will naturally have to
take into consideration the fact that the new firm will have to
fight against the hostility of the expelled partner, and consequently that there is a reasonable probability that their profits
may be less than had previously been the case.

Another class of case in which there is even more difficulty
at arriving at a fair estimate of the value of Goodwill is where
two partners have been carrying on business at two separate
places, and the partnership is being dissolved on terms that each
partner acquires the Goodwill of *one* business.   Here, of course,
in the nature of things, neither partner will afford the other
(*i.e.* the purchaser of the Goodwill) the benefit of his connections
or influence, and it may fairly be said—from one point of view
at least—that no question of Goodwill can arise ; but, on the
other hand, the probabilities are that the two businesses do not
earn profits in the same proportion as that in which the
partners were entitled to receive them, and that therefore some
adjustment becomes necessary when a dissolution is arranged
upon these lines.   In practice, however, such an adjustment is
less difficult than might, perhaps, at first sight have appeared,
inasmuch as it is only the amount (if any) by which the value
of the Goodwill acquired by one partner exceeds his due proportion of the value of *both* Goodwills that must be paid by him
to the other partner ; and if they are both valued upon the same
basis there is not room for any very wide difference of opinion
as to what the amount which must pass should be.

In most businesses it is the practice to base the value of the
Goodwill upon so many months' or years' purchase of the
average net profits of the business, but there are a few exceptions to this rule : for example, the Goodwill of licensed houses

is usually based upon the quantity of liquor purchased ; while the Goodwill of dairies is almost invariably based upon the quantity of milk bought ; and of butchers' shops upon the value of the meat sold. In each case the class of trade done and the prices earned are, of course, taken into account in arriving at an estimate of the *value* of the Goodwill ; but the real basis is the quantity of trade done, the profits earned thereon being a secondary consideration. There is much to be said in favour of this system of valuation in industries to which it can be applied, more particularly as it is frequently a far easier matter to verify the volume of the trade than the net profit actually earned ; but it is probably less for this reason that the system of quantities is adopted than because the amount of profit which may be earned upon such a turnover varies in many trades very considerably according to who is managing the business at the time. It should be borne in mind, however, that it is a much simpler matter to falsify the *volume* of trade done than to falsify the net profits earned in a consistent—and therefore a convincing—manner.

In the vast majority of cases the basis of valuation is the average net profits. This, however, is not the most reliable basis which could be employed, and this is a view which seems to be gaining ground, inasmuch as it is becoming more and more usual to take into consideration not only the amount of profits that have been earned in the past, but also the amount of capital which has had to be invested in order to earn those profits, and the amount of time and skill which the proprietors have had to expend in managing the undertaking in order to produce that result. These matters may, as a matter of account, readily be provided for by basing the Goodwill, not on the profits actually earned, but on the profits, less interest on capital, and less a provision estimated to represent the value of the management which has not already been charged against profits.

With regard to the desirability of taking into consideration the question of interest on capital, it seems unnecessary to say very much here, as it is probably generally admitted that a business that could produce an income of £500 per annum, upon a capital of £1,000, is far more valuable than one that will produce a like income, but involves the employment of a capital of £5,000. In order to arrive, therefore, at a basis upon which two such businesses can be compared, one must deduct from the profits in each case a sum representing (say) 5 per cent. interest on the average amount of actual capital employed in the businesses during the year when the profits were earned. Taking the two cases mentioned just now, it will be found that the business which employed £1,000 produced a profit of £450 after providing 5 per cent. interest on the capital employed, but that the business which required £5,000 to work it only produced a profit of £250 after providing for interest ; and (other things being even) the respective values of these two businesses would thus appear to be as 9 is to 5.

There is, however, a further factor to be taken into consideration, and that is that a business which requires its proprietor to expend in its management a considerable amount of time and skill is less valuable than one which will produce an equal income without any such expenditure. It is less valuable because, unquestionably, it will be found that in the open market it would realise less money ; but in addition to that (as a matter which would have to be taken into consideration in any disinterested valuation), it is important to remember that, when a man pays for Goodwill, *he pays for something that places him in the position of being able to earn more money than he would be able to earn by his own unaided exertions.* To take an extreme case, for instance, no man who places any value upon his time would pay anything for an undertaking which, after providing 5 per cent. interest on its capital, did not show a further profit in excess of the amount that the purchaser might be sure of earning anywhere else, without any capital outlay whatever.

The question of the tenure of the premises (where they happen to be a material factor in the Goodwill) must also be taken into account : if a short lease, whether there is any likelihood of renewal at a reasonable rent, and so on.

In order, therefore, to arrive at a real basis by which the value of one business can be compared with another, provision must be made, not only for interest on the capital employed, but also for the value of such services as have been rendered to that business by its proprietor, and not already been charged against profits. In the case of a business under management, where the proprietors do no work, no such reduction need, of course, be made ; but where the proprietors have to exercise a certain amount of supervision, it is necessary, in order to arrive at a real basis of comparison, to deduct from the profits, in addition to interest, a sum representing as nearly as may be the amount that the proprietor would have to pay a manager to do his work. It is often a very difficult matter to arrive at any reliable estimate of what this amount would be ; but, for such a purpose as this, it may be taken that, unless the concern be a very large one, involving a very considerable amount of skill and experience upon the part of the management, it would not be necessary to reckon the cost of management as being anything excessive. In most cases £500 per annum would be an outside figure ; while in many, perhaps, even £100 would be more than sufficient, particularly if the whole of the proprietor's time is not employed in the business. But if more than ordinary skill is required (as, for example in the case of most professions), then a very liberal allowance must be made under this head.

Returning, now, to the two cases previously cited, and applying this principle to them, let us further suppose that the business which employs £1,000 capital occupies a considerable portion of the proprietor's time, and that his services could not be replaced under £250 per annum; this reduces the actual profits for which a purchaser would be prepared to pay as Goodwill, from £500 to £200 per annum. On the other hand, in the second case mentioned, where a capital of £5,000 was required to earn a profit of £500, suppose that the business is under management, and that very little or no personal time of the proprietor need be expended thereon. It is, therefore, unnecessary to make any deduction except in respect of interest, and the purchaser would be prepared to pay on the basis that by acquiring the Goodwill of the undertaking, he acquires an income of £250, which he could not have obtained by his own unaided exertions. It would then appear that the respective values of the Goodwills of these two businesses is in the ratio of 4 to 5, and this is the fundamental basis upon which the Goodwill of a business should be valued.

But, having arrived at that basis, it is still necessary to consider how many months' or years' purchase of the surplus profits shown by the above method may fairly be asked for the Goodwill, as between a willing buyer and a willing seller. This is a matter upon which no rules can be laid down, as each individual case will possess special features that require to be taken into consideration before it is possible to arrive at a fair estimate of the value; but, among others, the following points would certainly claim attention :—

(1) Other things being even, the income which can be produced with the least capital outlay will command the highest Goodwill, even after interest on capital has been taken into consideration.

(2) Other things being even, a business which involves the least amount of skilled supervision upon the part of the proprietor will command the highest Goodwill.

(3) Income derived from a monopoly, or a quasi-monopoly, will command a higher rate of Goodwill than one derived from an industry in which competition is keen; but this hardly goes to the extent of attaching any special value to a business dealing in *patents*, unless, indeed, it seems improbable that any subsequent invention should make these patents practically valueless. Indeed, speaking in general terms, it is difficult to conceive of a *permanent* monopoly, and the ephemeral nature of such a business must, of course, in all cases be set off against its value while it lasts.

(4) A business which depends for the continuance of its prosperity upon its being carried on in the same place is really, so far as Goodwill is concerned, limited to the term for which the premises at present occupied are held; and, in the case of a business carrying on what is largely a "chance" trade upon premises held on a short lease, the value of the Goodwill is, for all practical purposes, only the value for an annuity for so many years; for, in addition to having to start again when the lease falls in, the business will then, in all probability, have to encounter the opposition of a competitor *occupying the old premises*. Or, should the purchaser be successful in securing a renewal of the lease, it would only be upon payment of an increased rent, or the expenditure of a large sum in permanent improvements. It is, therefore, very important in most cases to inquire as to the tenure upon which the business premises are held.

It will be seen that no hard and fast distinction has been drawn between "chance trade" and trade arising from connection. This view may seem a little surprising at first sight, but on further consideration it will be apparent that, so long as a certain amount of profit has been realised annually for a reasonable term, it matters very little indeed where it comes from, and that the disadvantage of not knowing one's customers is quite counterbalanced by the fact that one's customers do not know you, and so do not notice that there has been a change of proprietorship.

It is very difficult to formulate any general rules to arrange undertakings in classes of different value, inasmuch as different businesses carrying on the same industry will vary in value far more than different classes of industries; but it may be stated in general terms that the most valuable Goodwills are probably those of wholesale and retail traders whose income is derived chiefly from old-established connections; there is, however, a slight advantage in favour of wholesale trades, as many persons do not care to become "shopkeepers," and so there is a somewhat smaller demand for retail businesses. The Goodwill of a manufacturing business is generally less valuable, on account of the far larger amount of capital required, and also because competition is keener, and there is, as a rule, far less guarantee that an old-established house will continue to be prosperous after its founders have retired from the management. The Goodwill of a professional business is generally of less value still, on account of the great skill required to maintain its reputation; and, further, because, being of an almost purely personal nature, it is very difficult to guarantee that the whole of the connection will really pass to the purchaser. On the other hand, if the predominant partner still remains in the business, a professional connection is perhaps the most stable that can be found, and therefore the Goodwill of a *share* in a professional business will usually fetch as much as, if not more than, the Goodwill of a *share* of a manufacturing or a trading concern.

What is the precise number of years' purchase which may fairly be reckoned in each case is, as has been pointed out, a matter upon which it is very difficult to lay down any general rules ; but, so far as it is possible to give any general idea upon the subject, it may be stated that

The Goodwill of a wholesale or retail trading business is worth from one to five years' purchase ;

Of a manufacturing concern from one to four years' purchase ;

And of a professional concern from one to three years' purchase.

Newspapers and other quasi-monopolies will, of course, naturally command a very much higher price, ten years' purchase being a not exceptional figure.

In the case of both trading and manufacturing undertakings the Goodwill of a share (where the former proprietors still remain in the business, or where the more important of them still remain) would be at least 25 per cent. more than if the whole undertaking were acquired, while in the case of a profession it would be *at least twice as much.* With regard to professions, however, the principle does not apply in its entirety where there are several branches, each managed by a separate partner, who is comparatively unknown to the clients of the other branches.

In all cases, as has before been carefully pointed out, the basis of the number of years' purchase is the average net profits, less interest on the average capital employed, and less a reasonable sum to represent the remuneration of management.

All these estimates are supposed to be on the basis of an agreement between a willing seller and a willing buyer, under which the former agrees to do his utmost, by means of introductions, circulars, &c., to give the latter the full benefit of his connection, and they further presuppose that the purchaser acquires the right to use the old name. This question of the firm-name is one of paramount importance, it being probably the most valuable asset conveyed with the Goodwill, and representing quite half the value of the whole.   It is further assumed in all cases, not only that the retiring proprietor or partner is going out of the business in question, but also that he is going out of business.

Before leaving this question, it seems desirable to touch upon the question of the value of Goodwill in the case of a compulsory purchase, such as sometimes occurs when a partner is being bought out under circumstances provided for in the partnership agreement, or in cases when a firm or sole trader is being bought out for the purpose of a local authority effecting improvements, or a railway company acquiring the property.   The usual practice in these cases is to arrive at a valuation of what the Goodwill would be under normal circumstances, and to add to that amount a sum equal to 10 per cent. of such valuation, as further consideration in respect of the compulsory purchase.

In some cases, however, such as when land is acquired under compulsory powers, the Goodwill may remain the property of the trader, and any loss suffered by him in this event must be proved to be due to the removal of his place of business.   It will easily be understood that in some instances, even where premises are compulsorily acquired, the Goodwill of the trader may be purely personal, and not dependent on his place of abode, and therefore may suffer little or no deterioration in value.   Of course, where the removal does affect the value of the Goodwill—as it may easily do on account of the impossibility of finding other suitable premises in the locality—the trader would have the ordinary means of redress.

Upon the purchase of the Goodwill of an undertaking by a company, however, a different set of conditions obtains.   The shareholders of a company (*i.e.* the purchasers of the Goodwill in these cases) are not "workers" but investors, and therefore what they are prepared to pay for as Goodwill is the amount by which the probable dividends exceed the interest they could have earned upon their capital elsewhere. As, moreover, their liability is limited, they are prepared to pay at a higher rate than a purchaser would who adventured his whole fortune in the undertaking. The usual practice, therefore, is to base the Goodwill on the ordinary net profits (the investor's interest on capital being so low as to become a negligible quantity), and to compute the rate at about twice that which a private purchaser would be prepared to pay.

Where the Goodwill is paid for by the allotment of ordinary or deferred shares, it is, of course, obvious that holders of shares having prior rights are not prejudiced by the amount of such Goodwill being greater than would be obtainable from a sole trader, unless the shares having prior rights fall into line with the ordinary or deferred shares as regards capital in the event of winding-up.

In many cases it is to be feared that the investor, with his typical carelessness, does not trouble to make any inquiries as to the Goodwill of the concern for whose shares he subscribes. He is dazzled by the promoter's glowing words of wealth and wisdom, and fills up his application form without seriously thinking about the future, save perhaps in so far as it may be involved in the probable market price of the shares a few months hence. And when the annual accounts come to hand the item of Goodwill is either lumped together with half-a-dozen other assets, or smuggled away in some far corner where he is not likely to discover it.

CHAPTER IX.

THE FLUCTUATIONS OF GOODWILL.

WITH regard to the treatment of Goodwill in accounts, in the first instance it is desirable to draw the reader's attention to the fact that every business that is carried on at a profit possesses a Goodwill of *some* value, and that the value of that Goodwill will vary from time to time in direct relation to the profits which may on the average be earned.

If the profits of any business were to be recorded during a period in the form of a graph, then the value of its Goodwill, as based on the average profits, would be found to fluctuate in very much the same manner as the profits; but the fluctuation would not be so violent, on account of the fact that it would, under the usual practice, be based, not on the actual profits of any one period, but upon the average profits earned during a period of (say) three years ending on that date. On the other hand, the value of a Goodwill usually exceeds one year's purchase of the profits, and thus it is quite possible that the value of the Goodwill will actually fluctuate more than the value of the profits, and in any case the fluctuations will be quite at variance with what might be expected. In order to demonstrate more clearly what is meant in this connection, a graph is annexed, showing, so far as the thin line is concerned, the fluctuations in the profits of a business from year to year, while the two heavy lines show the corresponding value of the Goodwill based upon one year's purchase and two years' purchase respectively of the average profits for the past three years. The dotted thin line shows twice the profits, so that they may be compared with the upper heavy line.

GRAPH SHOWING RELATIVE FLUCTUATIONS in the PROFITS
of a BUSINESS and the VALUE of the GOODWILL when based
on the three years' average.

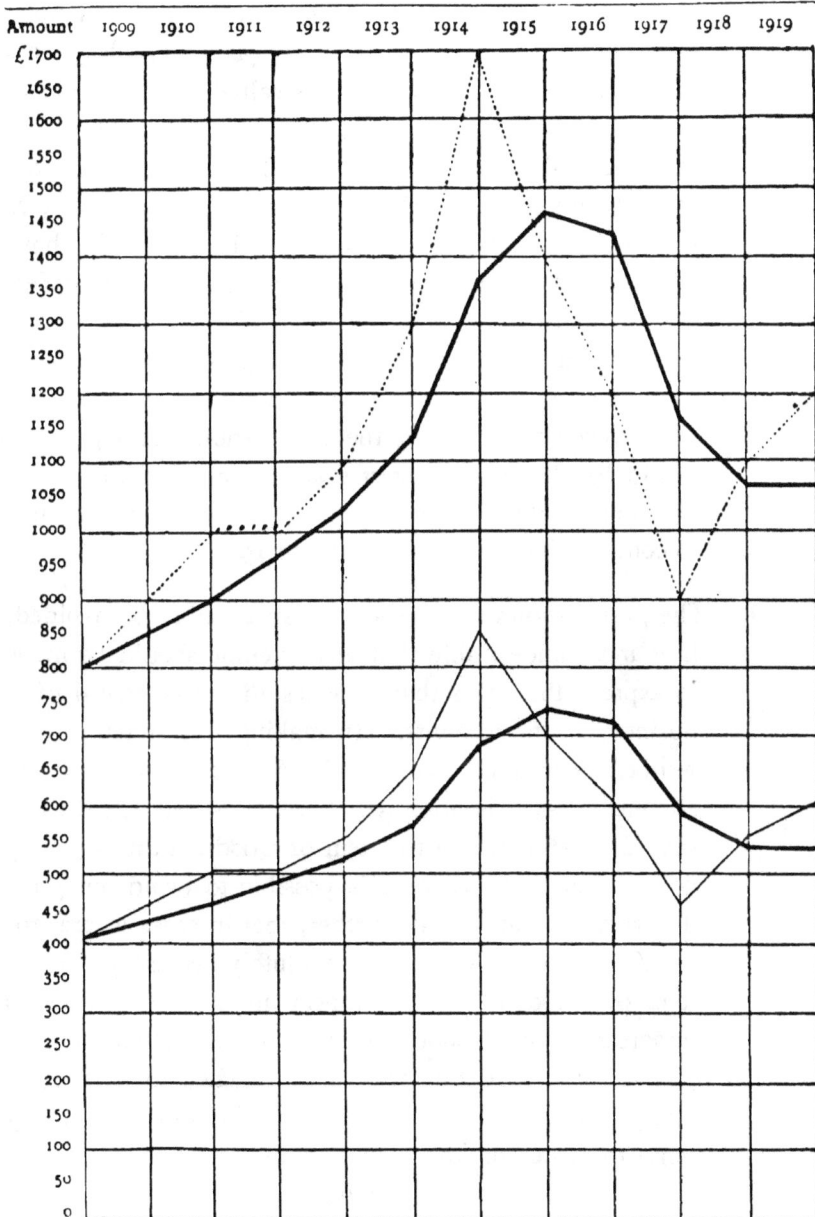

The reader has only to study this graph attentively to arrive at two irresistible conclusions :—

(1) That an average of any kind must not be relied upon implicitly. Thus, it is absurd to say (as the graph appears to show) that the Goodwill is less valuable than (say) two years' purchase of the profits while the latter are rising, and more valuable when they are falling. In many other respects this chart is well worthy of careful attention, as showing how careful it is necessary to be in applying hard and fast rules to matters arising in the course of professional experience. The true value of Goodwill is represented by the expectation of future profits, and the past profits are only of importance as helping one to forecast the future : thus, taking the graph shown over-page, it would be absurd to suggest that the value of the Goodwill was greatest at the end of 1915, and equally absurd to contend that it was declining in 1918.

(2) The graph shows that, when it can possibly be avoided, it is most undesirable that any attempt should be made to express the value that attaches to the Goodwill of a business in its accounts. In making this statement the writer is not unmindful of the fact that under many circumstances it is absolutely necessary that *some* value should be attached to the item of Goodwill ; it is merely pointed out that, where it is possible to avoid doing so, it is very desirable ; and, further, that in cases where, for some reason or another, it is absolutely necessary that the item of Goodwill should appear in the accounts, it is important that it should clearly be understood by all persons concerned that the value attached to it is absolutely arbitrary, and is not necessarily supposed in any sense to represent the actual value attached to Goodwill at the date of the accounts.

This latter statement may appear to the uninitiated to be somewhat startling, for there is, no doubt, a very general impression among those who are not very familiar with accounts that all the items set down on the right-hand side of a Balance Sheet are actual assets, and are stated at figures that are supposed to represent a reasonable estimate of their values at the date of the accounts. Certainly, so far as is reasonably practicable, the values of all "floating assets" should be stated in Balance Sheets on the basis of what they are actually worth to a going concern at the time of balancing, but it has been decided by Lord Justice Romer that in arriving at the profits of an undertaking it is incorrect to take into account fluctuations in the value of what his Lordship called "capital assets," and what accountants would call "fixed assets." There can be no question whatever but that Goodwill is a fixed asset, and not a floating asset; that is to say, it comes under the category of something which has to be acquired by an undertaking in order to enable it the better to carry on its business. Thus, there is a legal authority for holding the view that fluctuations in the value of Goodwill do not affect profits.

Accountants all know, however, that the ideas of lawyers on questions of account are not necessarily absolutely sound as expressions of unalterable principles, and it is, therefore, perhaps desirable to carry the argument to a point further, and to demonstrate the *undesirability* of taking into account any fluctuation in the value of Goodwill that may arise from time to time. This is a fallacy which may be very easily exposed. It may, perhaps, be an open question whether or not Goodwill can only be computed upon the balance of surplus profit arrived at after deducting interest on capital and cost of management; but, whatever the details of the process of valuation may be, it is incontestable that the value of a Goodwill from time to time will rise and fall as the profits earned increase or decrease. Assuming that a man with a capital of £5,000 is able to earn a profit (after debiting interest on capital and cost of management) of £1,000 per annum, and that his personal expenses amount to £500 per annum in excess of the amount he draws for interest and management, it is clear that as each year goes by his wealth will increase £500 per annum.   Supposing, however, the business is of such a nature that the Goodwill thereof is worth two years' purchase, is it to be seriously contended that, if at any time his profits increase to £1,500, and he is thus able to put by not £500, but £1,000 for the year, it is to be stated on the face of the accounts that his wealth has increased not merely £1,000 in respect of unspent profits, but also a further £1,000, as being two years' purchase of the increase representing enhanced Goodwill?   From one point of view, perhaps, this question may be answered in the affirmative, for it may be stated that the man's Capital Account should represent the worth of that which he has invested in the business ; but there is an overpowering argument in favour of the other view, namely, that the object of accounts is not merely to keep a record of profits earned in the business and of these profits alone, but also that everything in connection with such accounts is based upon the assumption that the undertaking is a going concern, and that, as a going concern, the value of the Goodwill, whether it go upwards or downwards, has no bearing upon the matter.   In other words, the value of Goodwill (or of a share thereof) does not crystallise until a sale takes place, and all attempts at an intermediate valuation are idle.

There is a further argument, however, in favour of disregarding fluctuations in Goodwill, in addition to the one that the immediate sale thereof is not a factor which is contemplated by anyone carrying on business, and that is that if the increase in its value be taken into account when the profits are good the effect will be to create the impression that the proprietors are doing from two to four times as well as is actually the case, and thus to encourage them to launch out in further personal expenditure upon a scale that they could not possibly maintain, and which even for a short period could only be met by realising at least a portion of that Goodwill—which, in plain English, amounts to much the same thing as "killing the goose that lays the golden eggs." *Per contra*, whenever times were bad, and there was a slight falling-off in the volume of profits, the effect of taking into consideration the decreased value of the Goodwill would be so to accentuate the unfortunate position as to discourage all but the most sanguine. Thus, apart from any questions of abstract principle, it will be seen that, from the point of view of mere expediency, it is most undesirable that these fluctuations of Goodwill should be allowed to enter into account at all.

Indeed, the only excuse for the insertion of such an item as Goodwill in accounts is that such an amount has actually been paid by the present proprietor for the Goodwill of the business. Thus, if one or more traders acquire a business as a going concern, and have paid a sum for Goodwill, they will probably expect to see in the accounts something representing the item "Goodwill" which they have actually paid for ; indeed, unless credit is taken for the value of the Goodwill, their capital, as stated in the accounts, is very much smaller than the actual amount which they personally have adventured in the undertaking, and this no doubt is (up to a point) a justification for the inclusion of this item in the accounts.

Similarly, in the case of a company acquiring an established business, a charge will no doubt have been made by the vendors in respect of Goodwill—probably upon the most liberal scale— and, as a matter of bookkeeping, it will then, under ordinary circumstances, be a physical impossibility to prevent the item of "Goodwill" from appearing as an asset in the accounts, as against the liability for Capital actually subscribed by the shareholders.

Another case in which the item of Goodwill may properly arise in accounts is where one of two or more partners retires, and is paid out by the remaining partners. When this is done, one of two courses becomes necessary : either the retiring partner must be paid out from the funds already existing in the business, or he must be paid out from funds contributed by the continuing partners, in addition to the capital which they have already adventured. In the former case, the continuing partners would hardly understand their respective shares of the Goodwill being debited to their Capital Accounts ; and, in the latter case, they would certainly not understand the credit balance of their Capital Accounts not being increased : therefore it is in many cases, perhaps, expedient that the value of the retiring partner's share should be stated in the accounts as an asset, so as to avoid disturbing the amounts standing to the credit of the continuing partner or partners. On the other hand, if it be admitted that the value attaching to Goodwill in accounts is, under ordinary circumstances, an arbitrary one, the same remark applies á fortiori when the value attached to the Goodwill represents only a fraction of the Goodwill ; and that being so, it seems clearly desirable that such an item should, if possible, be got rid of at once ; and, further, that so long as it is allowed to remain in the accounts, it should be clearly stated on the face of the Balance Sheet as representing the amount actually paid to a partner on his retirement.

It remains to consider the proper treatment in accounts when certain definite expenditure has been incurred by the proprietors of a business for the sake of *creating* a Goodwill. Thus, the expenditure incurred in advertising a new invention, in order to bring it prominently before the public, and the loss almost invariably incurred in starting a newspaper or the branch of a bank &c., may not improperly be debited, in the first instance, to '' Establishment Account '' ; and, in so far as these expenditures have been judicious, a residual value will doubtless remain

in respect of them which may fairly be treated as "Goodwill."
Indeed, it is generally desirable that some permanent record of
these expenses should be kept, and the Goodwill Account affords
a very convenient means of so doing. It is, however, chiefly in
respect of monopolies or quasi-monopolies that this principle
will be found applicable : advertising of an ordinary description
must only be capitalised (even temporarily) after the exercise of
the greatest caution.

In the nature of things a valuable Goodwill cannot be built
up without effort and sacrifice, and therefore necessarily involves
expenditure in the building up just as much as the purchase of
the Goodwill of an established business involves expenditure
upon the part of the purchaser. In the ordinary course of
events, it would be as impracticable as it would be undesirable
to attempt to keep an accurate account of the actual expenditure
incurred from time to time which might be treated as going to
build up a Goodwill hereafter. In all normal cases the natural
—and very clearly the best—course would be to treat all such
expenditure as chargeable against profits as and when incurred.

In certain cases, however, an exceptional treatment may be
justifiable :—

(1) Where it is clearly foreseen that the new undertaking must
necessarily be run at a loss before it can be built up into a profit-
earning concern, such initial Loss may be treated as the cost
incurred in establishing the Goodwill of the undertaking, and,
therefore, as a Capital item, instead of being treated as an
adverse balance on Profit and Loss Account, which must be
made good out of future profits before it can be said that the
undertaking has made profits available for distribution. This
treatment, of course, would not be permissible if it resulted in
leaving the undertaking with inadequate Working Capital to
continue operations, but assuming the undertaking has been able
to "turn the corner," and thus establish itself upon a profit-

earning basis, the assumption is that, after all initial Losses have been defrayed, there still remains an adequate balance of Working Capital.

(2) Where a new business has been established successfully upon a profit-earning basis as a result of Preliminary Advertising expenditure upon an extensive scale, clearly the above consideration applies with peculiar force, because in this case it is more practicable to distinguish between the expenditure actually incurred in the building up of the Goodwill and the expenditure necessarily incidental to the carrying on of the business from time to time. Whenever, however, expenditure upon Advertising is capitalised (whether the account to which it be debited be called " Goodwill Account " or by any other name) it is important to bear in mind that a business established by advertising will ordinarily require advertising for its maintenance. Clearly, recurring expenses cannot properly be regarded as Capital Expenditure. Only those expenses in connection with advertising, which it will not be necessary to repeat when once the undertaking has been firmly established, can properly be capitalised. Such expenses, however, may well be regarded as the actual ascertained cost of building up the Goodwill of the business.

CHAPTER X.

THE PURCHASE OF GOODWILL.

THE next point that claims consideration is the question as to how the item representing the actual cost of Goodwill should be dealt with in the accounts of a purchaser, or purchasers. With regard to the sole trader, or private firm, it seems unnecessary to lay down any definite rules, as the accounts are *their* accounts, and so long as they understand them nobody else is immediately concerned. But there is this important point to be considered ; it may happen at some future time that the existing proprietor or proprietors may wish to sell either the whole or a portion of the undertaking, and they will then find it necessary to produce accounts which, on the face of them, will show the amount that was at one time paid for the Goodwill of the undertaking. The chances are (at all events, if the business is an increasing one) that they will find it rather embarrassing to disclose this cost price at a subsequent date, and thus there is a very powerful argument in favour of the amount standing to the debit of Goodwill being written off with all convenient speed. Unquestionably, however, the amount should not be written off out of profits : it has no connection whatever with profits in the sense that it is of a wasting nature ; but none the less it is an asset which it is undesirable to retain as such, and the proper method of dealing with it clearly seems to be, at the earliest possible stage, to debit Capital Account and credit Goodwill Account with the whole amount of the Goodwill. Where there are two or more partners the proportion to be debited to each will, of course, be in accordance with their respective shares in the profits.

Coming now to the consideration of Goodwill in relation to the accounts of a company, there are two points to be considered.   In the first place all that has been said as to the undesirability of the cost price being retained as a permanent asset applies here; but, on the other hand, when the value of the Goodwill has been paid for out of *capital* it is practically impossible for it to be written off except out of profits, which (as has already been shown in the case of a private firm) is quite incorrect.   The expediency of writing it off by effecting a reduction of the company's capital is here disregarded for two reasons : in the first place, the cost of so doing would be a serious item which no one would willingly incur except for some tangible benefit; and, secondly, because as a matter of practice it is doubtful whether any Judge would sanction a reduction of capital on such grounds, the practice being for the Court to require to be satisfied that the capital had been *lost*, and, from a lawyer's point of view, it would hardly be considered that it had been lost in being expended on the Goodwill acquired, unless it could be proved that the Goodwill had actually become less valuable by reason of a decline in the profits earned.   As already stated, technically it would be incorrect to write down the amount of Goodwill out of profits ; it is true that in many of the soundest undertakings this process is adhered to, but it is thought that upon reflection it will be found to be radically wrong, and that what is really effected by the process is to create a Reserve Fund without stating it as such —or, in other words, a Secret Reserve.   There may be circumstances under which it is desirable that there should be such a Secret Reserve in existence, but in the vast majority of instances the chief object of a Reserve Fund is to parade it before the world as a proof of the financial stability of the company.   The only alternatives left, then, are for a company to maintain its Goodwill at the original cost (which is for many purposes undesirable in connection with a firm, and the same arguments apply to a company), or *not to pay for Goodwill out of capital.*

There are two ways for a company to acquire a Goodwill without paying for it out of capital; neither, however, is in very general use at the present time. The first and most usual method is by the creation of Founders' Shares; that is to say, the vendors of the Goodwill part with it, not for an immediate cash consideration, but for a few shares in the company, of a nominal value, which entitle them to a considerable proportion of the profits in the undertaking after a return has been made to the other shareholders which it is estimated is sufficient to cover the ordinary interest on capital. Before passing on to the second method, it is desirable to weigh the advantages which this method appears to possess. In the first place, it has the advantage of keeping out of the accounts the unsightly, un-wieldy, and " un-valuable " asset named " Goodwill "; but, against this, it has the disadvantage that, in the long run, if the Goodwill be of any real value, the vendors thereof are making a better bargain for themselves—and this for the simple reason that, instead of selling for cash, they are selling on results, and (as is well known) the cash buyer always gets the closest terms. The second disadvantage, from the point of view of the com-pany, is that, as a matter of practice, the holders of the Founders' Shares always stipulate for a voice in the manage-ment of the company, and for a share in the division of its assets in the event of a winding-up—usually no inconsiderable share—and it is only in the nature of things that whatever influence they are able to exert upon the management will be in favour of declaring large dividends whenever possible, no matter what arguments there might be (from the point of view of those who have risked their money in the undertaking) in favour of building up a large Reserve Fund. The holders of

Founders' Shares, as such, have practically no cash invested in the capital of the undertaking; their interest is entirely in declaring large dividends, not in building up the business so that it may last a great number of years and produce a fairly satisfactory result—indeed, to put it shortly, they would often sooner kill the golden goose than fatten it! As a matter of fact, however, this principle of Founders' Shares has, it is believed, never yet been applied where there was any really valuable and established Goodwill to be conveyed to a company. Where Founders' Shares exist they have generally been given as consideration to promoters of, or to those who have initiated *an idea*, out of which it was hoped that profits might be made in the future. A really valuable and old-established Goodwill is never conveyed to a company upon precisely these terms, although instances are not infrequent of the purchase-price consisting, in part or wholly, of a *large* issue of fully paid Founders' Shares; but— both from the point of view of the shareholders of the new company, and the vendors of the Goodwill of the undertaking to be acquired—the principle is not one that it is desirable to extend.

The alternative method for a company to acquire Goodwill without paying for it out of capital is one which, it is believed, has not yet been tried; yet it seems to be worthy of consideration, and it is now put forward as a suggestion, rather than as a statement of fact, or even as a statement of opinion to be accepted without fuller consideration. Before stating precisely what this alternative is, it is thought best to put this position of affairs before the reader. Upon an examination of the last published Balance Sheet of a certain company (which need not be named) it appears that the actual tangible assets are really worth £500,000, that the liabilities of the company are £200,000, its reserves and undivided profits £100,000, and its paid-up capital £200,000. It will thus be seen that for every pound which the existing shareholders have contributed there is

30s. value in the coffers of the company; yet the market price of the £1 shares is 50s. What, then, would buyers of these shares acquire for 50s. which is not represented by the 30s. just mentioned? The answer, of course, is that they would buy a proportionate share of the Goodwill of the undertaking, which apparently is valued (assuming at the moment—which is by no means always the case—that the Stock Exchange price is solely regulated by supply and demand) at 20s. per share. Does this not suggest a very simple method by which a company about to be formed might acquire the tangible assets and Goodwill of an undertaking? How would it be to let the share capital be fixed upon such a basis as to supply the necessary funds to acquire the tangible assets purchased, and provide a sufficient surplus for working capital; and in order to provide the necessary funds to acquire the Goodwill of the undertaking, let the shares be issued at such a premium as would amount to the price to be paid to the vendor for Goodwill?

There would appear on the face of it to be many advantages in such an arrangement, were it to become the recognised custom in connection with all company flotations. In the first place, the troublesome asset of Goodwill would be eliminated from the accounts altogether, and there would be no occasion to inquire as to how it was to be written off, or why it had not been written off, or what reserve there was against it, &c.; and, secondly, it would be apparent at the outset what tangible assets were acquired by the company, and separately what was paid for those intangible assets which are ordinarily represented under the convenient name of " Goodwill." On the other hand, it must be remembered that, whatever the apparent advantages of such a system may be, in practice there would always be a difficulty in getting the public to apply for shares at a premium in the case of a new and untried concern, and it is therefore feared that, in the particular form above suggested, the idea would be found unworkable. It seems, however, to be well worth considering whether something cannot be suggested that would appear to remove the difficulty (arising from the known lack of perception on the part of the British public) ; the best suggestion that occurs at the moment is that a portion of the paid-up capital should, from the outset, be allocated to the purchase of the Goodwill, and separately stated, upon the face of the Balance Sheet, "short," in the inner column, thereby obviating the necessity for any statement of the Goodwill on the assets side ; or it might be thought better to apply the double account system, and state these two items in a separate Balance Sheet for the sake of clearness, and certainly no one could then be misled.

One great advantage of some such innovation would be that whereas, at present, market prices are largely ruled by mere rumour, the published accounts of the various companies might then gradually be utilised for this purpose. At the present time it is practically impossible to trace any connection between a company's accounts and the price of its shares ; but were the above suggestion to be generally adopted, the premium on shares in the market (rigs being put on one side) should represent the current value of the Goodwill *plus* accumulated profits and reserves, while a fall below par should represent the diminution of the originally estimated value of the Goodwill, modified by any losses or accumulation of profits or reserves that might exist. Incidentally it may be mentioned that the mere fact that a company's shares were quoted at a discount would then imply that it had lost some of its tangible assets, as well as the whole of its Goodwill.

The facility which this method would afford of comparing the market price with the actual position of a company, as shown by its accounts, would, in course of time, no doubt be greatly appreciated by investors, and—by substituting fact for rumour, and knowledge for belief—it would tend to check extreme and unreasonable fluctuations in the market prices of shares. This would no doubt be an unqualified and most important advantage.

A great deal is heard from time to time concerning company law amendment, but it would seem that our legislators are keeping too much in one groove—and that not a very important one. Reform is wanted not so much in connection with either promoters, directors, or auditors as with shareholders themselves—in so far as they do not represent *bonâ fide* investors, but merely gamblers in differences on the rise and fall. In a very great number of companies these gamblers hold the voting power, and, that being so, everything has now to be arranged to suit their ends. Any reform, therefore, which would have the effect of discouraging *temporary* holdings in the shares of companies without interfering with their being readily marketable would be found to be for the ultimate advantage of the permanent shareholders in those companies, and it seems fairly evident this is really the chief point upon which the existing company law requires strengthening in order to protect *bonâ fide* investors. Anything which would have the effect of reducing the fluctuations in shares would naturally tend to produce this result, while the mere fact that the shares of almost all companies stood at a premium would have at least a tendency to reduce speculative buying.

The vast majority of the companies that fail within a very short time of their inception, fail on account of the enormous price which has been charged for the undertaking by the vendor, which price would never have been paid if shareholders had seen the items they were buying and the prices they were paying for each. This is a fact which is sufficiently proved by the reports of the Comptroller of the Companies Department. If some such suggestion as that which has been sketched out were to be adopted, and such portion of the purchase-price as did not represent tangible assets (or the excess of tangible assets over liabilities) were to be issued in the form of a premium upon shares, investors would, before they parted with their money, be in possession of at least the most material fact in connection with each individual matter.   If the price charged for Goodwill were excessive, it is probable that the public would not subscribe for the issue; and surely this would be infinitely more to the advantage of the community than any inquiry which could afterwards be made as to why the company in question had failed to earn profits for its shareholders sufficient to pay a dividend upon the "watered" capital?   It has rightly been stated that no company law can be enacted through which a clever company promoter cannot drive a coach and four; but if the difficulties which have been pointed out could be overcome, and it were enacted that anything intangible acquired by a company had to be paid for out of premiums on shares issued (the nominal value of the shares being only in respect of tangible assets), a very large number of the worst cases of failure and fraud would be put a stop to on their inception, and unless such matters can be put a stop to at the start there is little or no good in interfering at all.

In view of the practice—which in certain quarters is regarded with great favour—of making further issues of capital *pro rata* to existing shareholders at less than their current market value, it seems desirable to state in the clearest possible language that the inevitable and necessary effect of such a procedure is to depreciate the value of the shares.   Thus, supposing a company with a capital of £50,000 in shares of £1 each is desirous of raising a further £20,000, and suppose further that its shares stand at 1¼ in the market : then, in the opinion of the market, the value of that company's assets (including Goodwill) exceeds its liabilities by £12,500, or there would be no basis for valuing its 50,000 shares at £62,500.   Then, if 20,000 further shares be issued at par, the surplus will be increased to £82,500; but this now represents the basis of value for 70,000 shares, so the value of each share is 1 3/16, representing a fall of 1/16 as a result of this ill-advised issue. If, instead of issuing 20,000 new shares at par, the company had issued 16,000 new shares at a premium of $\frac{1}{4}$, its surplus assets would still have been £82,500; but its total issue would have been 66,000 shares, and the facts would thus have justified the continuance of the price of the shares at $1\frac{1}{4}$. All shares issued at less than their intrinsic value are practically issued at a discount : the process is equivalent to taking a partner into a business without asking him to pay for his share of the Goodwill at its current market value.

In a leading article, *The Times* (20th March 1905) pointed out that " a Goodwill is valuable only as long as a com- " pany is doing well ; the directors cannot borrow on its security " when bad times come, and if the worst comes to the worst, " and liquidation is necessary, its selling value will, *ex hypothesi*, " have vanished almost completely." It is further remarked, in support of the elimination of Goodwill from a Balance Sheet, that " nothing should be reckoned as an asset which cannot be taken to a bank as security for an advance." A point is made that in those well-financed concerns where Goodwill *is* shown as an asset on the Balance Sheet, there is always a substantial reserve on the other side, capable in most cases of absorbing the " undesirable contra." Our contemporary's desire to see Goodwill either clearly and fairly stated on a company's Balance Sheet, or removed altogether, is laudable, and its indignation at the practice of hiding the Goodwill under some omnibus form of wording, so that its existence amongst the solid assets may not be apparent, is certainly well founded. Such a practice can only be described as sheer jugglery, for which there can be no excuse.

The example given by our contemporary—namely, the London United Tramways Company, whose Goodwill was said to be stowed away among " tramways and light railway under-takings, properties, and equipment "—is interesting, but it is curious that while the White Star Line is spoken of with favour by *The Times* in the same article, Mr. S. S. Dawson, F.C.A., has stated that "the basis of the purchase of the White Star "Line by the American financiers was ten years' purchase of a "given year's profits, but for this sum not only the Goodwill of "the fleet but the fleet itself was acquired—not upon a basis of "either cost, or independent valuation of the steamers."

It should not be overlooked that any writing down of Goodwill out of profits, unless it be to correct an actual shrinkage in value since the date when the Goodwill was acquired, is *pro tanto* the setting aside of a secret reserve.

There does not, however, appear to be any valid reason, where a company takes over a business as and from an earlier date than that on which it was entitled to commence business and the profits are apportioned accordingly, why that section of the profits which has been carried to a special Capital Reserve Account should not be used for the purpose of writing down the Goodwill. Indeed, this would appear to be the most desirable course to pursue. The price of Goodwill has doubtless been inflated because the vendors agreed to forego accruing profits.

CHAPTER XI.

GOODWILL IN PARTNERSHIP ACCOUNTS.

It is now proposed to deal with various problems affecting Goodwill which arise in practice, and it is thought that these can best be demonstrated by showing their effect upon the Balance Sheet. Since it is an accepted axiom of accounting that the proper recording of any and every business transaction does not disturb the equilibrium of the balance, however much the constituent parts of that balance may be affected, a succession of Balance Sheets following each step in the record appears to be a more concise way of illustrating cause and effect than full entries and Ledger Accounts, which would be more suited to a work devoted entirely to bookkeeping.

The first case considered is that of a sole trader who is admitting a partner. The following Balance Sheet is presumed to record the position of Mr. John Smith as on the 30th June 1920 :—

JOHN SMITH.

BALANCE SHEET (A), 30th June 1920.

Liabilities.	£	s	d	Assets.	£	s	d	£	s	d
Capital Account :—				Stock-in-Trade				5,000	0	
John Smith	9,045	0	0	Book Debts	8,200	0	0			
Sundry Creditors	5,000	0	0	Deduct Reserve for						
				Doubtful Debts ..	820	0	0			
								7,380	0	0
				Cash at Bank	1,650	0	0			
				„ in Hand	15	0	0			
								1,665	0	0
	£14,045	0	0					£14,045	0	0

It is supposed that he has come to an arrangement with Mr. T. Jones, whereby he admits the latter into partnership as from the 1st July 1920 upon the terms of Jones paying in £3,000 in cash for a fifth share in the business, subject to the Stock being taken at a discount of 5 per cent. and the Book Debts at a discount of 7½ per cent.   The first step will naturally be to reconstruct the Balance Sheet of John Smith as on the 30th June, on the basis of the amended figures, as per his agreement with Jones.

JOHN SMITH.

BALANCE SHEET (B), 30th June 1920.

Liabilities.	£ s d	£ s d
Capital Account:—		
John Smith	9,045 0 0	
Add Reserve for Doubtful Debts written back..	820 0 0	
	9,865 0 0	
Deduct Amount written off Stock £250 0 0		
Reserve for Doubtful Debts .. 615 0 0		
	865 0 0	
		9,000 0 0
Sundry Creditors		5,000 0 0
		£14,000 0 0

Assets.	£ s d	£ s d	£ s d
Stock-in-Trade	5,000 0 0		
Deduct Amount written off	250 0 0		
		4,750 0 0	
Book Debts	8,200 0 0		
Deduct Reserve for Doubtful Debts ..	615 0 0		
		7,585 0 0	
Cash at Bank ..	1,650 0 0		
in Hand ..	15 0 0		
		1,665 0 0	
			£14,000 0 0

Jones is now admitted, and it is supposed that he has had to pay £1,000 for a fifth share of the Goodwill and the remaining £2,000 as capital. Having discovered, however, that the (whole) Goodwill is to be valued at £5,000 (£1,000 × 5 = £5,000), Smith's position must first be shown under the new conditions :—

JOHN SMITH.

BALANCE SHEET (C), 30th June 1920.

Liabilities.	£ s d	£ s d	Assets.	£ s d	£ s d
Capital Account:—			Sundry Assets, as per Balance Sheet B) ..		14,000 0 0
John Smith, as per Balance Sheet (B)	9,000 0 0		Goodwill		5,000 0 0
Add Goodwill, as per contra	5,000 0 0				
		14,000 0 0			
Sundry Creditors..		5,000 0 0			
		£19,000 0 0			£19,000 0 0

Jones then pays £3,000 into the business, and the position becomes as follows :—

SMITH & JONES.
BALANCE SHEET (D), 1st July 1920.

Liabilities.	£ s d	£ s d	Assets.	£ s d	£ s d
Capital Accounts:—			Goodwill		5,000 0 0
John Smith, as per Balance Sheet (C)	14,000 0 0		Stock-in-Trade		4,750 0 0
T. Jones	3,000 0 0		Book Debts	8,200 0 0	
		17,000 0 0	Deduct Reserve for Doubtful Debts ..	615 0 0	
Sundry Creditors		5,000 0 0			7,585 0 0
			Cash at Bank ..	4,650 0 0	
			Do. in hand ..	15 0 0	
					4,665 0 0
		£22,000 0 0			£22,000 0 0

It will be noticed that in the Balance Sheet here shown (D)
the item of Goodwill appears at the full face value of £5,000.
On the other hand it is considered (generally speaking) undesirable that the item should appear in books of account.   There is
no reason whatever why it should not at once be written off to
the Capital Accounts of Smith and Jones.   If it is so written off,
it must, of course, be debited to their respective Capital Accounts
in the same proportions as they bear profits and losses; that is
to say, four-fifths must be charged against Smith's Capital
Account, and one-fifth to Jones's Capital Account.   The position will then be :—

SMITH & JONES.

BALANCE SHEET (E), 1st July 1920.

Liabilities.	£ s d	£ s d	£ s d
Capital Accounts:—			
J. Smith	14,000 0 0		
Deduct Share of Goodwill written off	4,000 0 0		
		10,000 0 0	
T. Jones	3,000 0 0		
Deduct Share of Goodwill written off	1,000 0 0		
		2,000 0 0	
Sundry Creditors		5,000 0 0	
		£17,000 0 0	

Assets.	£ s d	£ s d	£ s d
Stock-in-Trade			4,750 0 0
Book Debts	8,200 0 0		
Deduct Reserve for Doubtful Debts ...	615 0 0		
			7,585 0 0
Cash at Bank ...	4,650 0 0		
Do. in hand ...	15 0 0		
			4,665 0 0
			£17,000 0 0

N.B.—It will be observed that, although Smith and Jones share profits and losses in the ratios of 4 : 1, their respective capitals are not in these ratios. The capital to be introduced by each partner is always a matter of arrangement between them.

It is now worth while to call attention to another manner in which this might have been given effect to.

It has been thought more desirable to show in detail what may be called the " full " record of the transactions ; but it will be seen that what Jones has really agreed to do is to pay £1,000 to Smith for one-fifth share of the Goodwill, and to put £2,000 cash into the business ; Smith, on the other hand, agreeing to put into the business his assets and liabilities at the agreed valuations, together with the £1,000 which Jones has paid him.

This might really have been more simply recorded in the books of Smith and Jones had the £9.000 standing to the credit of Smith in his old books (see Balance Sheet (B)) been left to his credit in the books of the new firm.   Then Jones might pay £3,000 into the bank, £2,000 in his own name, and £1,000 in the name of Smith, which would be posted to their respective Capital Accounts.   Had the Balance Sheet been taken out upon these lines, it would have appeared as follows :—

SMITH & JONES.

BALANCE SHEET (F), 1st July 1920.

Liabilities.	£ s d	£ s d
Capital Accounts:—		
John Smith, as per Balance Sheet (B) £9,000 0 0		
Add Amount paid him by T. Jones 1,000 0 0	10,000 0 0	
T. Jones	2,000 0 0	
		12,000 0 0
Sundry Creditors..		5,000 0 0
		£17,000 0 0

Assets.	£ s d	£ s d
Stock-in-Trade		4,750 0 0
Book Debts	8,200 0 0	
Deduct Reserve for Doubtful Debts ..	615 0 0	
		7,585 0 0
Cash at Bank ..	4,650 0 0	
Do. in hand ..	15 0 0	
		4,665 0 0
		£17,000 0 0

In such a case as the preceding, as Smith's share of the profits is four-fifths, it might be thought preferable that his capital should not exceed £8,000 (four-fifths of the capital of the firm). If the remaining £2,000 were required for the purposes of the business, it could be advanced by Smith to the firm as a loan.

———

The next case to be considered is that of two partners, already in business, admitting a third.

A. and B., sharing profits in ratio of two to one, agreed to admit C. on payment of £600 for a one-third share in the business and £2,000 as capital. The position of A. and B. on 30th June 1920 was as follows :—

A. & B.

BALANCE SHEET (1), 30th June 1920.

Liabilities.	£ s d		Assets.	£ s d
Capital Accounts :—			Sundry Assets (details are not given, as they are not material to the points to be considered)	8,500 0 0
A. £5,000 0 0				
B... .. .. 2,000 0 0				
	7,000 0 0			
Sundry Creditors ..	1,500 0 0			
	£8,500 0 0			£8,500 0 0

The first step will be to reconstruct the Balance Sheet of A. and B. so as to show the Goodwill.

A. & B.

BALANCE SHEET (2), 30th June 1920.

Liabilities.	£ s d	£ s d	Assets.	£ s d
Capital Accounts:—			Sundry Assets (see Balance Sheet (1))	8,500 0 0
A. £5,000 0 0			Goodwill (on basis of £600 for a one-third share) ..	1,800 0 0
Add Share of Goodwill 1,200 0 0	6,200 0 0			
B. 2,000 0 0				
Add Share of Goodwill.. 600 0 0	2,600 0 0			
		8,800 0 0		
Sundry Creditors		1,500 0 0		
		£10,300 0 0		£10,300 0 0

C. is then admitted, paying £2,600 into the funds of the partnership.

The following Balance Sheet shows the effect of the admission :—

A., B. & C.

BALANCE SHEET (3), 1st July 1920.

Liabilities.	£ s d	£ s d	Assets.	£ s d	£ s d
Capital Accounts:—			Sundry Assets	8,500 0 0	
A.	6,200 0 0		*Add* Cash paid in by C.	2,600 0 0	
B.	2,600 0 0				11,100 0 0
C. ..	2,600 0 0		Goodwill ..		1,800 0 0
		11,400 0 0			
Sundry Creditors		1,500 0 0			
		£12,900 0 0			£12,900 0 0

The partners share profits as follows:—

A. $\frac{4}{9}$ B. $\frac{2}{9}$ C. $\frac{3}{9}$.

Since the retention of the Goodwill in the books (and therefore in the Balance Sheet) of the partnership is undesirable, the position after writing off the Capital Accounts of the partners will be :—

A., B. & C.

BALANCE SHEET (4), 1st July 1920.

Liabilities	£ s d	£ s d	Assets	£ s d
Capital Accounts :—			Sundry Assets as per Balance Sheet (3)	11,100 0 0
A., as per Balance Sheet (3) £6,200 0 0				
Deduct Share of Goodwill written off 800 0 0	5,400 0 0			
B., as per Balance Sheet (3) 2,600 0 0				
Deduct Share of Goodwill written off 400 0 0	2,200 0 0			
C., as per Balance Sheet (3) 2,600 0 0				
Deduct Share of Goodwill written off 600 0 0	2,000 0 0	9,600 0 0		
Sundry Creditors		1,500 0 0		
		£11,100 0 0		£11,100 0 0

As before, £2,733 6s. 8d. of A.'s capital, and £866 12s. 4d. of B.'s, might be transferred to Loan Account, if desired.

Following our first illustration, if the Goodwill had been omitted from the accounts of A. and B. (see Balance Sheet (1) page 116), and the amount paid by C. as Goodwill credited to their Capital Accounts in the proportions in which they then shared profits and losses, the position would have been :—

A., B. & C.

BALANCE SHEET (5), 1st July 1920.

Liabilities.	£ s d	£ s d	£ s d
Capital Accounts :—			
A. £5,000 0 0			
Add Proportion of Premium paid by			
C. .. : 400 0 0		5,400 0 0	
B. 2,000 0 0			
Add Proportion of Premium paid by			
C. .. : 200 0 0		2,200 0 0	
			9,600 0 0
Sundry Creditors ..			1,500 0 0
			£11,100 0 0

Assets.	£ s d	£ s d	£ s d
Sundry Assets .. .. :	8,500 0 0		
Add Cash paid in by C... :	2,600 0 0		
		11,100 0 0	
			£11,100 0 0

As a further illustration, let us suppose that A. and B. approached C. on the basis of Balance Sheet (2)—that is, with the Goodwill in the books of account—and offered him a third share in the business, on the terms that £600 were to be paid privately to them and £2,000 placed in the business as capital. On acceptance the position would be :—

A., B. & C.

BALANCE SHEET (6), 1st July 1920.

Liabilities.	£ s d	£ s d	Assets.	£ s d	£ s d
Capital Accounts:—			Sundry Assets	8,500 0 0	
A.	6,200 0 0		Add Amount paid in by C.	2,000 0 0	
B.	2,600 0 0				10,500 0 0
C.	2,000 0 0		Goodwill..		1,800 0 0
		10,800 0 0			
Sundry Creditors		1,500 0 0			
		£12,300 0 0			£12,300 0 0

In the elimination of the Goodwill in this case, care should be taken to see that it is written off in the proportion in which the *old* partners shared profits.   The resultant sharing will be :—

A., B. & C.

BALANCE SHEET (7), 1st July 1920.

Liabilities.	£ s d	£ s d		Assets.	£ s d	£ s d
Capital Accounts :—				Sundry Assets	8,500 0 0	
A. £6,200 0 0				*Add* Cash paid in by C...	2,000 0 0	
Deduct Share of Goodwill written off 1,200 0 0	5,000 0 0					10,500 0 0
B 2,600 0 0						
Deduct Share of Goodwill written off 600 0 0	2,000 0 0					
C.	2,000 0 0					
		9,000 0 0				
Sundry Creditors ..		1,500 0 0				
		£10,500 0 0				£10,500 0 0

It will be observed that A. and B. are not prejudiced because they, in fact, received £600 privately from C., which they shared in the proportion in which they bore profits and losses —namely, two-thirds and one-third—and therefore A. will have received £400 and B. £200; and if these sums be mentally added to the balance of their respective Capital Accounts as per Balance Sheet (7), it will be seen that their position is not really distinct from that indicated in Balance Sheet (5).

The next illustration deals with the circumstances arising out of the death of a partner.

X., Y. & Z. were in partnership, sharing profits and losses in the ratio of 5, 3, and 4. The Articles of Partnership provided (*inter alia*) that on the death of a partner the Goodwill of the business was to be valued on the basis of the average annual profits for the three years preceding the decease of the partner, and purchased by the survivors. Z. died on 30th June 1920. (All questions of profit, of interest on capital, or drawings are disregarded as being beyond the scope of the present work.) Suppose the position, after adjusting all these matters, to be as follows :—

X., Y. & Z.

BALANCE SHEET (A), 30th June 1920.

Liabilities.	£ s d	£ s d	*Assets.*	£ s d
Capital Accounts :—			*Sundry Assets (not including	
X.	.. 5,000 0 0		Goodwill)	14,000 0 0
Y.	.. 3,000 0 0			
Z.	.. 4,000 0 0			
		12,000 0 0		
Sundry Creditors		2,000 0 0		
		£14,000 0 0		£14,000 0 0

---

* If this item included something for Goodwill, already appearing in the books of the partnership, the adjustments shown over-page would be in respect of the *difference* between the two Goodwill figures, and might be either upwards or downwards.

The Goodwill, valued in accordance with the terms of the Articles of Partnership, amounted to £2,400. The final position, therefore, showing amount due to executors of Z. would be :—

X., Y. & (Z).

BALANCE SHEET (B), 30th June 1920.

Liabilities.	£ s d	£ s d	£ s d	Assets.	£ s d
Capital Accounts :—				Sundry Assets	14,000 0 0
X. £5,000 0 0				Goodwill	2,400 0 0
Add Share of Goodwill.. .. .. 1,000 0 0		6,000 0 0			
Y. 3,000 0 0					
Add Share of Goodwill 600 0 0		3,600 0 0			
			9,600 0 0		
Amount due to Executors of Z.:—					
Balance of Capital Account ..	4,000 0 0				
Add Share of Goodwill ..	800 0 0				
		4,800 0 0			
Sundry Creditors ..			2,000 0 0		
			£16,400 0 0		£16,400 0 0

If X. and Y. pay out the executors of Z., and write off the Goodwill, the Balance Sheet would require adjustment in the following manner :—

X. & Y

BALANCE SHEET (C), 1st July 1920

Liabilities.	£ s d	£ s d
Capital Accounts :—		
X. £6,000 0 0		
Deduct Share of Goodwill (⅓), written off .. 1,500 0 0	4,500 0 0	
Y. 3,600 0 0		
Deduct Share of Goodwill (⅓), written off .. 900 0 0	2,700 0 0	
		7,200 0 0
Sundry Creditors		2,000 0 0
		£9,200 0 0

Assets.	£ s d	£ s d
Sundry Assets as per Balance Sheet (B)	£14,000 0 0	
Deduct amount realised and paid to Executors of Z.	4,800 0 0	
		9,200 0 0
		£9,200 0 0

The above illustration will, of course, serve in the case of the retirement, instead of the death, of a partner.

As an example of the proper treatment where one partner retires and another takes his place, the following may be cited :—

D., E., and F. were partners, sharing profits and losses in the ratio of 4, 2, and 2. Their position on 30th June 1920 was as indicated in the Balance Sheet set out below :—

D., E. & F.

BALANCE SHEET (1). 30th June 1920.

Liabilities.	£	s	d	£	s	d	Assets.	£	s	d	£	s	d
Capital Accounts :—							Sundry Assets ..				15,000	0	0
D.	6,000	0	0										
E.	3,000	0	0										
F.	3,000	0	0	12,000	0	0							
Sundry Creditors..				3,000	0	0							
				£15,000	0	0					£15,000	0	0

F. was about to retire, and D. and E. agreed to assume G. in his place, on the terms that he paid to F. the sum ultimately found to be due to him, and also a further sum of £1,000 for a third share of the business. In order to find the amount due to F. it is first of all necessary to reconstruct the Balance Sheet by inserting the Goodwill.

D., E. & F.

BALANCE SHEET (2), 30th June 1920.

Liabilities.	£	s	d	£	s	d	*Assets.*	£	s	d
Capital Accounts:—							Sundry Assets	15,000	0	0
D.	£6,000	0	0				Goodwill ..	3,000	0	0
Add Share of Goodwill ..	1,500	0	0	7,500	0	0				
E.	3,000	0	0							
Add Share of Goodwill ..	750	0	0	3,750	0	0				
F.	3,000	0	0							
Add Share of Goodwill ..	750	0	0	3,750	0	0				
				15,000	0	0				
Sundry Creditors ..				3,000	0	0				
				£18,000	0	0		£18,000	0	0

G. now brings in £4,750 as per agreement, and the **position** changes to—

D., E., (F.) & G.
BALANCE SHEET (3), 30th June 1920.

Liabilities.	£ s d	£ s d	Assets.	£ s d	£ s d
Capital Accounts:—			Sundry Assets	15,000 0 0	
D. .. :: ::	7,500 0 0		*Add* Cash paid in by G.	4,750 0 0	
E. .. :: ::	3,750 0 0				19,750 0 0
F. .. :: ::	3,750 0 0		Goodwill ..		3,000 0 0
G. .. :: ::	*4,750 0 0				
		19,750 0 0			
Sundry Creditors		3,000 0 0			
		£22,750 0 0			£22,750 0 0

* Unless the contrary be clearly specified in the terms of the arrangement, G. is entitled to receive credit for the full £4,750.

F. is then paid out :—

D., E. & G.

BALANCE SHEET (4), 30th June 1920.

Liabilities.	£ s d	£ s d	Assets.	£ s d	£ s d
Capital Accounts:—			Sundry Assets	19,750 0 0	
D.	7,500 0 0		Deduct Amount paid to F. ..	3,750 0 0	
E.	3,750 0 0				16,000 0 0
G.	4,750 0 0		Goodwill ..		3,000 0 0
		16,000 0 0			
Sundry Creditors		3,000 0 0			
		£19,000 0 0			£19,000 0 0

The Goodwill is now written off in the new proportions.

D., E. & G.

BALANCE SHEET (5), 1st July 1920.

Liabilities.	£ s d	£ s d	Assets.	£ s d
Capital Accounts:—			Sundry Assets	.. 16,000 0 0
D. £7,500 0 0				
Deduct Share of Good-will (⅛) written off .. 1,333 6 8		6,166 13 4		
E. 3,750 0 0				
Deduct Share of Good-will (⅛) written off .. 666 13 4		3,083 6 8		
G. 4,750 0 0				
Deduct Share of Good-will (⅛) written off .. 1,000 0 0		3,750 0 0		
		13,000 0 0		
Sundry Creditors		3,000 0 0		
		£16,000 0 0		£16,000 0 0

The reader is invited to very carefully contrast these various accounts, so that he may be quite sure that he appreciates the differences which occur under the various methods.

CHAPTER XII.

GOODWILL IN COMPANIES' ACCOUNTS.

THE next point that appears to claim detailed attention is the different modes of presenting, in the form of a Balance Sheet, the position of affairs of a company formed to acquire a business at a price including something for the Goodwill of the undertaking. The following example represents the Balance Sheet of the " X. Y. Z." Company, Lim., as at the 1st of January 1920, prepared upon the usual lines, the Goodwill being stated as an asset to the value of £5,000, for the acquiring of which share capital has had to be issued :—

" X. Y. Z." COMPANY LIMITED.

BALANCE SHEET 1st January 1920.

Liabilities.	£ s d	Assets.	£ s d
Nominal Capital £30,000 0 0		Goodwill	5,000 0 0
		Freehold Premises	10,000 0 0
Capital Subscribed, viz. :—·		Plant and Machinery	5,000 0 0
25,000 Ordinary Shares of £1		Stock-in-Trade	5,000 0 0
each	25,000 0 0	Cash at Bank	4,000 0 0
Debentures	4,000 0 0		
	£29,000 0 0		£29,000 0 0

The same position of affairs would be recorded in the following manner, if instead of the capital subscribed being 25,000 shares of £1 each (making a paid-up capital of £25,000) issued at par, 20,000 shares of £1 each had been issued at a premium of 5s. per share, the premiums upon these shares—amounting in all to £5,000—having been applied to the purchase of the Goodwill without the latter appearing upon the face of the accounts as such :—

" X. Y. Z." COMPANY LIMITED.

BALANCE SHEET 1st January 1920.

Liabilities.	£ s d	Assets.	£ s d
Nominal Capital £30,000 0 0		Freehold Premises ..	10,000 0 0
		Plant and Machinery ..	5,000 0 0
Capital Subscribed, viz. :—		Stock-in-Trade	5,000 0 0
20,000 Ordinary Shares of		Cash at Bank	4,000 0 0
£1 each (issued at 5s.			
per share premium, the			
premium being applied to			
the purchase of the Good-			
will of the undertaking)..	20,000 0 0		
Debentures	4,000 0 0		
	£24,000 0 0		£24,000 0 0

Exception may be taken to the above form, upon the ground that it does not sufficiently fully set out the amount of premium received upon shares, nor the amount paid for Goodwill. These objections may be overcome by adopting the form of Balance Sheet shown over-page, in which it will be seen that the amount of premiums on shares is stated in an inner column upon the liabilities side of the Balance Sheet, with the addition of an explanation that this amount has been applied to the purchase of the Goodwill of the undertaking. If the further objection should be raised that the Goodwill, having been purchased, should be stated upon the assets side of the Balance Sheet, this may be met by so stating it in an inner column as a *contra* entry

to the premiums upon shares ; but it has not been thought necessary to adopt this course in the following example :—

" X. Y. Z." COMPANY LIMITED.

BALANCE SHEET 1st January 1920.

Liabilities.	£. s d	Assets.	£ s d
Nominal Capital £30,000 0 0		Freehold Premises	10,000 0 0
		Plant and Machinery	5,000 0 0
Capital Subscribed, viz. :—		Stock-in-Trade	5,000 0 0
20,000 Ordinary Shares of £1 each	20,000 0 0	Cash at Bank	4,000 0 0
Premiums on Shares (applied to the purchase of the Goodwill of the undertaking) .. £5,000 0 0			
Debentures	4,000 0 0		
	£24,000 0 0		£24,000 0 0

The only points which it appears desirable to draw attention
in the above Balance Sheet are—

The item Goodwill, which appears at £13,800 ; namely,
£3,300, as being the agreed value of the Goodwill of the " A."
Company, and £10,500, the agreed value of the Goodwill of
the " B." Company, as before stated.

It will be seen that the items " Reserve Fund " and " Profit
and Loss Account " in the Balance Sheet of the " B." Company
do not appear in the Balance Sheet of the amalgamated company ; while of the subscribed capital of 69,000 ordinary shares
of £1 each, 20,000 will have been issued as fully-paid to the
shareholders of the " A." Company, and 49,000 as fully-paid
to the shareholders of the " B." Company, who thus get 7 new
shares for each 5 old shares held by them.

The above Balance Sheet of the " A. & B. (United), Lim.,"
is framed upon the usual lines, that is to say, the Goodwill is

included as an asset at the actual cost to the undertaking; but it may be pointed out that, following upon the procedure already mentioned, it would have been a simple matter to have placed this £13.800 in an inner column upon the assets side, and a corresponding amount of the subscribed capital in an inner column; so that the total of the assets side of the Balance Sheet would then only show the actual tangible assets of the under-taking.   Or, had the method been adopted of issuing the shares of the " A. & B. (United), Lim.," at a premium that would have sufficed to provide the £13.800 paid by the company for the Goodwill of the undertakings of the " A." and " B." Com-panies, then by a simple calculation it will be found that the " A. & B. (United), Lim.," ought to have issued its shares at a premium of 5s. per share.   Had this been done, the paid-up capital (including premiums) of £69,000 could have been obtained by the issue of 55,200 shares of £1 each at a premium of 5s., and the position could then have been recorded as shown in the following example :—

THE " A. & B. (UNITED)," LIMITED.

BALANCE SHEET, 30th June 1920.

Liabilities.	£ s d	Assets.	£ s d
Nominal Capital £60,000 0 0		Freehold and Leasehold Premises	12,000 0 0
Subscribed Capital, viz. :—		Plant and Machinery ..	11,900 0 0
55,200 Ordinary Shares of		Stock-in-Trade	14,000 0 0
£1 each	55,200 0 0	Book Debts	17,500 0 0
Premiums on Issue of Shares (applied to Purchase of Goodwill) .. £13,800 0 0		Cash at Bank	9,300 0 0
Sundry Creditors	9,500 0 0		
	£64,700 0 0		£64,700 0 0

The foregoing example deals with the question of Goodwill by showing the premium on the issue of shares by way of memorandum upon the liabilities, stating that this premium has been applied to the purchase of the Goodwill of the undertaking. If thought desirable, a corresponding entry could, of course, have been made in respect of this Goodwill upon the assets side, the amount being stated " short," so as not to be included in the total of the tangible assets acquired.

Had this method been adopted, 16,000 ordinary shares of £1 each would be allotted to the shareholders of the " A." Company, Lim., for the purpose of acquiring their undertaking, and the balance of 39,200 ordinary shares of £1 each would have been issued as fully-paid to the shareholders of the " B." Company.

Throughout it has been assumed that the purchasing company has accepted the values stated for *all* the assets of both vendor companies. If any of the values be not admitted, and yet the purchasing company is willing to pay the same purchase-price, it follows that the difference must be thrown on to the valuation of Goodwill.

The effect of issuing new shares in a company *pro rata* to existing shareholders at a price appreciably below the current market price of the existing shares is not generally understood. Accordingly, it has been thought worth while to deal with the matter here. It cannot be too clearly stated that all such issues necessarily involve " watering " the Capital of the company. Their necessary and inevitable effect is to reduce the value of the old shares to an amount in the aggregate precisely equal to the bonus ostensibly given to the shareholders in connection with the new issue.

This, like the other matters explained here, may be best shown by the aid of an illustration. Let us suppose that the following Balance Sheet represents the position of the R.S.T. Co., Lim., on the 31st December 1919, and that upon that date the market price of this company's shares was 30/-. Market price is, of course, not necessarily exactly the same thing as true value. Market price (which is continually fluctuating) is the result of buying and selling orders given to brokers by persons who, for the most part, are only very imperfectly acquainted with the circumstances of the case and, therefore, quite incompetent to judge the actual value of the shares for the time being. It would perhaps illustrate the principle which it is sought here to elucidate better, if the proposition were that "the *value* of this company's shares on 31st December 1919 was 30/-," but it would be as well not to let this point—interesting as it is—divert our attention from the main issue.

R. S. T. Co. Limited.
Balance Sheet (1) 31st December 1919.

Liabilities.	£	£ s d	*Assets.*	£ s d
Nominal Capital ..	100,000		Sundry Assets (possibly, but not necessarily, including "Goodwill")	85,000 0 0
Subscribed Capital—				
50,000 Shares of £1 each ..	50,000	0 0		
Sundry Creditors	20,000	0 0		
Reserve Fund	10,000	0 0		
Profit and Loss Account ..	5,000	0 0		
		£85,000 0 0		£85,000 0 0

Let us suppose that the R. S. T. Co.. Lim., on 31st December 1919 offered 25,000 shares *pro rata* to its existing shareholders **at par,** and that the whole issue was taken up, whereupon its Balance Sheet would appear as follows :—

R. S. T. Co. Limited.
Balance Sheet (2) 1st January 1920.

Liabilities.	£ s d	£ s d	*Assets.*	£ s d	£ s d
Nominal Capital ..	100,000 0 0		Sundry Assets—		
Subscribed Capital—			As before	85,000 0 0	
75,000 Shares of £1 each ..		75,000 0 0	*Add* proceeds of issue of 25,000		
Sundry Creditors		20,000 0 0	new shares of £1		
Reserve Fund		10,000 0 0	each at par ..	25,000 0 0	
Profit and Loss Account.. ..		5,000 0 0			110,000 0 0
		£110,000 0 0			£110,000 0 0

To go back a step. As shown in Balance Sheet (1) the assets of the company at 31st December 1919 amounted to £85,000, according to the books of the company, and its external liabilities to £20,000. Thus, according to the books, the net property of the shareholders was worth £65,000. If, however, the value of one share was 30/-, the value of the 50,000 shares then issued was £75,000. In the opinion of " the market," therefore, the position of the company was £10,000 more favourable than its Balance Sheet shows, owing possibly to Goodwill not appearing in the Balance Sheet at all, or appearing in the Balance Sheet at less than what it was supposed to be actually worth. Or, on the other hand, the difference of £10,000 may be due in part or in whole to the belief that the other assets in the Balance Sheet are undervalued, or that the item " Sundry Creditors " includes various Reserves which in point of fact will never materialise. However that may be, it is clear that, if the value of one share be 30/-, the value of £50,000 shares is regarded as being £75,000, and not £65,000.

Balance Sheet (2), which is supposed to have been prepared after the new Capital had been issued, shows assets standing at £110,000, and external liabilities (as before) at £20,000, leaving a net amount of £90,000. If we add to this the sum of £10,000—the amount by which Balance Sheet (1) (and therefore also Balance Sheet (2)) is supposed to understate the actual position—we arrive at a figure of £100,000 supposed to represent the actual value of the property possessed by the shareholders. The holders of each of the 75,000 issued shares is accordingly entitled to $\frac{1}{75000}$ of £100,000, i.e. to £1 6s. 8d. It will be seen therefore that the effect of issuing new shares has been to average down, or to " water," the value of the old shares— as is indeed necessary to compensate for the fact that each of the £25,000 new shares that has been issued having equal rights to the old shares and is therefore worth more than the issue price of 20/-.

The problem would have been more complex had the new shares been as of a different class from the old shares, but the same principle would necessarily hold good. Whenever the new shares are worth more than the price of issue, the bonus involved in their issue has necessarily to be paid for by the holders of the old shares, who accordingly experience a corresponding decline in the value of their property. The effect may not be instantaneous as judged by the market price of the shares, because, as already stated, market prices are to a very large extent influenced by buying and selling orders given by persons unacquainted with all the circumstances; but sooner or later it is inevitable that the truth should make itself felt, and that the market price of the shares fall. This tendency may, however, be mitigated by the fact that the company is able to turn its new capital to such good use as thereby materially to increase the value of the Goodwill of its business.

What holds good with regard to new shares issued *pro rata* to existing shareholders, naturally applies also to issues to promoters, underwriters and others. The effect in all cases is that the old shareholders have to pay a bonus to the new allottees, although naturally the true nature of the transaction is not disclosed by the accounts of the company.

There seems to be no reason why a similar method of stating the position of affairs in the Balance Sheet should not be adopted, even when the shares have not been issued at a premium; thus, supposing in the case of the "X. Y. Z." Company, Lim., the undertaking had been acquired from the vendors by the payment of £25,000, of which £10,000 had been paid in cash and £15,000 in fully-paid shares, then these £15,000 of shares issued as fully paid might be subdivided upon the Balance

Sheet, showing that 5,000 of such shares had been issued for the purpose of acquiring the Goodwill of the undertaking, these shares being inserted in an inner column as shown in the example given upon page 140.   It might, of course, be argued that, if this method were adopted, the paid-up capital of the company would not be very clearly set forth; but this by no means necessarily follows.   It would be perfectly possible to follow out the lines indicated above, and yet show in the plainest possible manner what was the amount of capital issued and paid up.

"X. Y. Z." COMPANY LIMITED.

BALANCE SHEET, 1st January 1920.

Liabilities.	£ s d	£ s d
Nominal Capital :—		
10,000 Ordinary Shares of £1 each £30,000 0 0		
Subscribed Capital :—		
20,000 Ordinary Shares of £1 each, devoted to the purchase of the undertaking, and the provision of Working Capital	20,000 0 0	
5,000 Ordinary Shares of £1 each, devoted to the purchase of the Goodwill	5,000 0 0	
		25,000 0 0
Debentures .—		
40 Bonds of £100 each bearing interest at 5 per cent.		4,000 0 0
		£29,000 0 0

Assets.	£ s d
Goodwill	5,000 0 0
Freehold Premises	10,000 0 0
Plant and Machinery ..	5,000 0 0
Stock-in-Trade	5,000 0 0
Cash at Bank	4,000 0 0
	£29,000 0 0

It is now proposed to show the best method of dealing with the question of Goodwill when the businesses owned by two existing companies are acquired by a third company, formed for the purpose of amalgamating these two. The same principles, of course, apply equally if, instead of the businesses of *existing* companies being acquired, the undertakings purchased are those of firms or private individuals. The following is supposed to be the Balance Sheet of the " A." Company, Lim., one of the undertakings to be acquired by the new company; it will be seen that the subscribed capital of this company is £20,000, and that the value placed upon the Goodwill in the Balance Sheet is £3.300 :—

THE " A " COMPANY LIMITED.

BALANCE SHEET, 30th June 1920.

Liabilities.	£ s d	Assets.	£ s d
Nominal Capital £20,000 0 0		Goodwill	3,300 0 0
		Freehold Premises ..	8,500 0 0
Capital Subscribed, viz. :—		Plant and Machinery ..	3,500 0 0
20,000 Ordinary Shares of		Stock-in-Trade	3,500 0 0
£1 each	20,000 0 0	Cash at Bank	3,700 0 0
Sundry Creditors	2,500 0 0		
	£22,500 0 0		£22,500 0 0

The second undertaking proposed to be acquired by the new company is that of the " B." Company, Lim., whose paid-up capital amounts to £35,000, there being also a Reserve Fund of £2,800 and an unappropriated balance on Profit and Loss Account of £700. Nothing appears upon the face of the Balance Sheet of the " B." Company for the value of the Goodwill of the undertaking. This Balance Sheet is as follows :—

THE "B" COMPANY LIMITED.
BALANCE SHEET, 30th June 1920.

Liabilities.	£ s d	Assets.	£ s d
Nominal Capital £50,000 0 0		Leasehold Premises	3,500 0 0
		Plant and Machinery	8,400 0 0
Subscribed Capital, viz. :—		Stock-in-Trade	10,500 0 0
35,000 Ordinary Shares of		Book Debts	17,500 0 0
£1 each	35,000 0 0	Cash at Bank	5,600 0 0
Reserve Fund	2,800 0 0		
Sundry Creditors	7,000 0 0		
Profit and Loss Account ..	700 0 0		
	£45,500 0 0		£45,500 0 0

For the purpose of arriving at a basis of amalgamation, let it be assumed that the agreed value of shares in the " A." Company is " par," and that the shares in the " B." Company are worth 28s. apiece, and, further, that the scheme of amalgamation is that they shall be acquired by the new company at these prices, payable in shares of that new company, the " A. & B. (United), Lim."

If the shares of the " B " Company are worth 28s. apiece it follows that the aggregate value of the whole of the share capital is £49,000. Having arrived at this figure, and proceeding upon the lines already laid down, it is a simple matter for us to frame the Balance Sheet of the " A. & B. (United), Lim.," assuming that it has acquired the undertakings of the " A." Company and the " B." Company upon the above terms. This Balance Sheet appears as follows :—

THE "A. & B. (UNITED)" LIMITED.
BALANCE SHEET, 30th June 1920.

Liabilities.	£ s d	Assets.	£ s d
Nominal Capital £100,000 0 0		Goodwill	13,800 0 0
		Freehold and Leasehold	
Subscribed Capital, viz. :—		Premises	12,000 0 0
69,000 Ordinary Shares at		Plant and Machinery ..	11,900 0 0
£1 each	69,000 0 0	Stock-in-Trade	14,000 0 0
Sundry Creditors	9,500 0 0	Book Debts	17,500 0 0
		Cash at Bank	9,300 0 0
	£78,500 0 0		£78,500 0 0

APPENDIX A.

THE TRADE MARKS ACT, 1905.

(5 Edw. VII., c. 15.)

An Act to consolidate and amend the law relating to trade marks.

[11th August 1905.]

BE it enacted by the King's most Excellent Majesty, by and with the advice and consent of the Lords Spiritual and Temporal, and Commons, in this present Parliament assembled, and by the authority of the same, as follows :—

1.—This Act may be cited as the Trade Marks Act, 1905.

2.—This Act shall, save as otherwise expressly provided, come into operation on the first day of April one thousand nine hundred and six.

PART I.

Definitions.

3.—In and for the purposes of this Act (unless the context otherwise requires) :—

A "mark" shall include a device, brand, heading, label, ticket, name, signature, word, letter, numeral, or any combination thereof :

A "trade mark" shall mean a mark used or proposed to be used upon or in connection with goods for the purpose of indicating that they are the goods of the proprietor of such trade mark by virtue of manufacture, selection, certification, dealing with, or offering for sale :

A "registrable trade mark" shall mean a trade mark which is capable of registration under the provisions of this Act :

" The register " shall mean the Register of Trade Marks kept under
the provisions of this Act :

A "registered trade mark " shall mean a trade mark which is
actually upon the register :

"Prescribed" shall mean, in relation to proceedings before the
Court, prescribed by rules of Court, and, in other cases, prescribed by this Act or the Rules thereunder :

"The Court " shall mean (subject to the provisions for Scotland,
Ireland, and the Isle of Man) His Majesty's High Court of
Justice in England.

Register of Trade Marks.

4.—There shall be kept at the Patent Office for the purposes of this
Act a book called the Register of Trade Marks, wherein shall be
entered all registered trade marks with the names and addresses of
their proprietors, notifications of assignments and transmissions, dis-
claimers, conditions, limitations, and such other matters relating to
such trade marks as may from time to time be prescribed. The register
shall be kept under the control and management of the Comptroller-
General of Patents, Designs, and Trade Marks, who is in this Act
referred to as the Registrar.

5.—There shall not be entered in the register any notice of any trust
expressed, implied, or constructive, nor shall any such notice be receiv-
able by the Registrar.

6.—The Register of Trade Marks existing at the date of the commencement of this Act, and all Registers of Trade Marks kept under
previous Acts, which are deemed part of the same book as such
register, shall be incorporated with and form part of the register.
Subject to the provisions of sections thirty-six and forty-one of this
Act, the validity of the original entry of any trade mark upon the
registers so incorporated shall be determined in accordance with the
statutes in force at the date of such entry, and such trade mark shall
retain its original date, but for all other purposes it shall be deemed
to be a trade mark registered under this Act.

7.—The register kept under this Act shall at all convenient times be
open to the inspection of the public, subject to such regulations as
may be prescribed ; and certified copies, sealed with the seal of the
Patent Office, of any entry in any such register shall be given to any
person requiring the same on payment of the prescribed fee

Registrable Trade Marks.

8.—A trade mark must be registered in respect of particular goods or classes of goods.

9.—A registrable trade mark must contain or consist of at least one of the following essential particulars :—

(1) The name of a company, individual, or firm represented in a special or particular manner ;

(2) The signature of the applicant for registration or some predecessor in his business ;

(3) An invented word or invented words ;

(4) A word or words having no direct reference to the character or quality of the goods, and not being according to its ordinary signification a geographical name or a surname ;

(5) Any other distinctive mark, but a name, signature, or word or words, other than such as fall within the descriptions in the above paragraphs (1), (2), (3), and (4), shall not, except by order of the Board of Trade or the Court, be deemed a distinctive mark ;

Provided always that any special or distinctive word or words, letter, numeral, or combination of letters or numerals used as a trade mark by the applicant or his predecessors in business before the thirteenth day of August one thousand eight hundred and seventy-five, which has continued to be used (either in its original form or with additions or alterations not substantially affecting the identity of the same) down to the date of the application for registration shall be registrable as a trade mark under this Act.

For the purposes of this section " distinctive " shall mean adapted to distinguish the goods of the proprietor of the trade mark from those of other persons.

In determining whether a trade mark is so adapted, the tribunal may, in the case of a trade mark in actual use, take into consideration the extent to which such user has rendered such trade mark in fact distinctive for the goods with respect to which it is registered or proposed to be registered.

10.—A trade mark may be limited in whole or in part to one or more specified colours, and in such case the fact that it is so limited shall be taken into consideration by any tribunal having to decide on the distinctive character of such trade mark. If and so far as a trade mark is registered without limitation of colour it shall be deemed to be registered for all colours.

11.—It shall not be lawful to register as a trade mark or part of a trade mark any matter, the use of which would by reason of its being calculated to deceive or otherwise be disentitled to protection in a Court of Justice, or would be contrary to law or morality, or any scandalous design.

Registration of Trade Marks.

12.—(1) Any person claiming to be the proprietor of a trade mark who is desirous of registering the same must apply in writing to the Registrar in the prescribed manner.

(2) Subject to the provisions of this Act the Registrar may refuse such application, or may accept it absolutely or subject to conditions, amendments, or modifications.

(3) In case of any such refusal or conditional acceptance the Registrar shall, if required by the applicant, state in writing the grounds of his decision and the materials used by him in arriving at the same, and such decision shall be subject to appeal to the Board of Trade or to the Court at the option of the applicant.

(4) An appeal under this section shall be made in the prescribed manner, and on such appeal the Board of Trade or the Court, as the case may be, shall, if required, hear the applicant and the Registrar, and shall make an order determining whether, and subject to what conditions, amendments, or modifications, if any, the application is to be accepted.

(5) Appeals under this section shall be heard on the materials so stated by the Registrar to have been used by him in arriving at his decision, and no further grounds of objection to the acceptance of the application shall be allowed to be taken by the Registrar, other than those stated by him, except by leave of the tribunal hearing the appeal. Where any further grounds of objection are taken the applicant shall be entitled to withdraw his application without payment of costs on giving notice as prescribed.

(6) The Registrar or the Board of Trade or the Court, as the case may be, may at any time, whether before or after acceptance, correct any error in or in connection with the application, or may permit the applicant to amend his application upon such terms as they may think fit.

13.—When an application for registration of a trade mark has been accepted, whether absolutely or subject to conditions, the Registrar shall, as soon as may be after such acceptance, cause the application as accepted to be advertised in the prescribed manner. Such advertisement shall set forth all conditions subject to which the application has been accepted.

14.—(1) Any person may, within the prescribed time from the date of the advertisement of an application for the registration of a trade mark, give notice to the Registrar of opposition to such registration.

(2) Such notice shall be given in writing in the prescribed manner, and shall include a statement of the grounds of opposition.

(3) The Registrar shall send a copy of such notice to the applicant, and within the prescribed time after the receipt of such notice, the applicant shall send to the Registrar, in the prescribed manner, a counter-statement of the grounds on which he relies for his application, and, if he does not do so, he shall be deemed to have abandoned his application.

(4) If the applicant sends such counter-statement, the Registrar shall furnish a copy thereof to the persons giving notice of opposition, and shall, after hearing the parties, if so required, and considering the evidence, decide whether, and subject to what conditions, registration is to be permitted.

(5) The decision of the Registrar shall be subject to appeal to the Court or, with the consent of the parties, to the Board of Trade.

(6) An appeal under this section shall be made in the prescribed manner, and on such appeal the Board of Trade or the Court, as the case may be, shall, if required, hear the parties and the Registrar, and shall make an order determining whether, and subject to what conditions, if any, registration is to be permitted.

(7) On the hearing of any such appeal any party may either in the manner prescribed or by special leave of the tribunal bring forward further material for the consideration of the tribunal.

(8) In proceedings under this section no further grounds of objection to the registration of a trade mark shall be allowed to be taken by the opponent or the Registrar other than those stated by the opponent as herein-above provided except by leave of the tribunal hearing the appeal. Where any further grounds of objection are taken the applicant shall be entitled to withdraw his application

without payment of the costs of the opponent on giving notice as prescribed.

(9) In any appeal under this section, the tribunal may, after hearing the Registrar, permit the trade mark proposed to be registered to be modified in any manner not substantially affecting the identity of such trade mark, but in such case the trade mark as so modified shall be advertised in the prescribed manner before being registered.

(10) The Registrar, or in the case of an appeal to the Board of Trade, the Board of Trade shall have power in proceedings under this section to award to any party such costs as they may consider reasonable, and to direct how and by what parties they are to be paid.

(11) If a party giving notice of opposition or of appeal neither resides nor carries on business in the United Kingdom, the tribunal may require such party to give security for costs of the proceedings before it relative to such opposition or appeal, and in default of such security being duly given may treat the opposition or appeal as abandoned.

15.—If a trade mark contains parts not separately registered by the proprietor as trade marks, or if it contains matter common to the trade or otherwise of a non-distinctive character, the Registrar or the Board of Trade or the Court, in deciding whether such trade mark shall be entered or shall remain upon the register, may require, as a condition of its being upon the register, that the proprietor shall disclaim any right to the exclusive use of any part or parts of such trade mark, or of all or any portion of such matter, to the exclusive use of which they hold him not to be entitled, or that he shall make such other disclaimer as they may consider needful for the purpose of defining his rights under such registration : Provided always that no disclaimer upon the register shall affect any rights of the proprietor of a trade mark except such as arise out of the registration of the trade mark in respect of which the disclaimer is made.

16.—When an application for registration of a trade mark has been accepted and has not been opposed, and the time for notice of opposition has expired, or having been opposed the opposition has been decided in favour of the applicant, the Registrar shall, unless the Board of Trade otherwise direct, register the said trade mark, and the trade mark, when registered, shall be registered as of the date of the application for registration, and such date shall be deemed for the purposes of this Act to be the date of registration.

17.—On the registration of a trade mark the Registrar shall issue to the applicant a certificate in the prescribed form of the registration of such trade mark under the hand of the Registrar, and sealed with the seal of the Patent Office.

18.—Where registration of a trade mark is not completed within twelve months from the date of the application by reason of default on the part of the applicant, the Registrar may, after giving notice of the non-completion to the applicant in writing in the prescribed manner, treat the application as abandoned unless it is completed within the time specified in that behalf in such notice.

Identical Trade Marks.

19.—Except by order of the Court or in the case of trade marks in use before the thirteenth day of August one thousand eight hundred and seventy-five, no trade mark shall be registered in respect of any goods or description of goods which is identical with one belonging to a different proprietor which is already on the register with respect to such goods or description of goods, or so nearly resembling such a trade mark as to be calculated to deceive.

20.—Where each of several persons claims to be proprietor of the same trade mark, or of nearly identical trade marks in respect of the same goods or description of goods, and to be registered as such proprietor, the Registrar may refuse to register any of them until their rights have been determined by the Court, or have been settled by agreement in a manner approved by him or (on appeal) by the Board of Trade.

21.—In case of honest concurrent user or of other special circumstances which, in the opinion of the Court, make it proper so to do, the Court may permit the registration of the same trade mark, or of nearly identical trade marks, for the same goods or description of goods by more than one proprietor subject to such conditions and limitations, if any, as to mode or place of user or otherwise, as it may think it right to impose.

Assignment.

22.—A trade mark when registered shall be assigned and transmitted only in connection with the Goodwill of the business concerned in the goods for which it has been registered and shall be determinable with that Goodwill. But nothing in this section contained shall be deemed to affect the right of the proprietor of a registered trade mark to assign the right to use the same in any British possession or protectorate or foreign country in connection with any goods for which it is registered together with the Goodwill of the business therein in such goods.

23.—In any case where from any cause, whether by reason of dissolution of partnership or otherwise, a person ceases to carry on business, and the Goodwill of such person does not pass to one successor but is divided, the Registrar may (subject to the provisions of this Act as to associated trade marks), on the application of the parties interested, permit an apportionment of the registered trade marks of the person among the persons in fact continuing the business, subject to such conditions and modifications, if any, as he may think necessary in the public interest. Any decision of the Registrar under this section shall be subject to appeal to the Board of Trade.

Associated Trade Marks.

24.—If application be made for the registration of a trade mark so closely resembling a trade mark of the applicant already on the register for the same goods or description of goods as to be calculated to deceive or cause confusion if used by a person other than the applicant, the tribunal hearing the application may require as a condition of registration that such trade marks shall be entered on the register as associated trade marks.

25.—If the proprietor of a trade mark claims to be entitled to the exclusive use of any portion of such trade mark separately he may apply to register the same as separate trade marks. Each such separate trade mark must satisfy all the conditions and shall have all the incidents of an independent trade mark, except that when registered it and the trade mark of which it forms a part shall be deemed to be associated trade marks and shall be entered on the register as such, but the user of the whole trade mark shall for the purposes of this Act be deemed to be also a user of such registered trade marks belonging to the same proprietor as it contains.

26.—When a person claiming to be the proprietor of several trade marks for the same description of goods which, while resembling each other in the material particulars thereof, yet differ in respect of—

(a) Statements of the goods for which they are respectively used or proposed to be used; or

(b) Statements of number, price, quality, or names of places; or

(c) Other matter of a non-distinctive character which does not substantially affect the identity of the trade mark; or

(d) Colour;

seeks to register such trade marks, they may be registered as a series in one registration. All the trade marks in a series of trade marks so registered shall be deemed to be, and shall be registered as, associated trade marks.

27.—Associated trade marks shall be assignable or transmissible only as a whole and not separately, but they shall for all other purposes be deemed to have been registered as separate trade marks. Provided that where under the provisions of this Act user of a registered trade mark is required to be proved for any purpose, the tribunal may if and so far as it shall think right accept user of an associated registered trade mark, or of the trade mark with additions or alterations not substantially affecting its identity, as an equivalent for such user.

Renewal of Registration.

28.—The registration of a trade mark shall be for a period of fourteen years, but may be renewed from time to time in accordance with the provisions of this Act.

29.—The Registrar shall, on application made by the registered proprietor of a trade mark in the prescribed manner and within the prescribed period, renew the registration of such trade mark for a period of fourteen years from the expiration of the original registration or of the last renewal of registration, as the case may be, which date is herein termed " the expiration of the last registration."

30.—At the prescribed time before the expiration of the last registration of a trade mark, the Registrar shall send notice in the prescribed manner to the registered proprietor at his registered address of the date at which the existing registration will expire and the conditions as to payment of fees and otherwise upon which a renewal of such registration may be obtained, and if at the expiration of the time prescribed in that behalf such conditions have not been duly complied with, the Registrar may remove such trade mark from the register, subject to such conditions (if any) as to its restoration to the register as may be prescribed.

31.—Where a trade mark has been removed from the register for non-payment of the fee for renewal, such trade mark shall, nevertheless, for the purpose of any application for registration during one year next after the date of such removal, be deemed to be a trade mark which is already registered, unless it is shown to the satisfaction of the Registrar that there had been no *bonâ fide* trade user of such trade mark during the two years immediately preceding such removal.

Correction and Rectification of the Register.

32.—The Registrar may, on request made in the prescribed manner by the registered proprietor or by some person entitled by law to act in his name,—

(1) Correct any error in the name or address of the registered proprietor of a trade mark; or

(2) Enter any change in the name or address of the person who is registered as proprietor of a trade mark; or

(3) Cancel the entry of a trade mark on the register; or

(4) Strike out any goods or classes of goods from those for which a trade mark is registered; or

(5) Enter a disclaimer or memorandum relating to a trade mark which does not in any way extend the rights given by the existing registration of such trade mark.

Any decision of the Registrar under this section shall be subject to appeal to the Board of Trade.

33.—Subject to the provisions of this Act where a person becomes entitled to a registered trade mark by assignment, transmission, or other operation of law, the Registrar shall, on request made in the prescribed manner, and on proof of title to his satisfaction, cause the name and address of such person to be entered on the register as proprietor of the trade mark. Any decision of the Registrar under this section shall be subject to appeal to the Court or, with the consent of the parties, to the Board of Trade.

34.—The registered proprietor of any trade mark may apply in the prescribed manner to the Registrar for leave to add to or alter such trade mark in any manner not substantially affecting the identity of the same, and the Registrar may refuse such leave or may grant the same on such terms as he may think fit, but any such refusal or conditional permission shall be subject to appeal to the Board of Trade. If leave be granted, the trade mark as altered shall be advertised in the prescribed manner.

35.—Subject to the provisions of this Act—

(1) The Court may on the application in the prescribed manner of any person aggrieved by the non-insertion in or omission from the register of any entry, or by any entry made in the register without sufficient cause, or by any entry wrongly remaining on the register, or by any error or defect in any entry in the register, make such order for making, expunging, or varying such entry, as it may think fit :

(2) The Court may in any proceeding under this section decide any question that it may be necessary or expedient to decide in connection with the rectification of the register :

(3) In case of fraud in the registration or transmission of a registered trade mark, the Registrar may himself apply to the Court under the provisions of this section :

(4) Any order of the Court rectifying the register shall direct that notice of the rectification shall be served upon the Registrar in the prescribed manner who shall upon receipt of such notice rectify the register accordingly.

36.—No trade mark which is upon the register at the commencement of this Act and which under this Act is a registrable trade mark shall be removed from the register on the ground that it was not registrable under the Acts in force at the date of its registration. But nothing in this section contained shall subject any person to any liability in respect of any act or thing done before the commencement of this Act to which he would not have been subject under the Acts then in force.

37.—A registered trade mark may, on the application to the Court of any person aggrieved, be taken off the register in respect of any of the goods for which it is registered, on the ground that it was registered by the proprietor or a predecessor in title without any *bonâ fide* intention to use the same in connection with such goods, and there has in fact been no *bonâ fide* user of the same in connection therewith, or on the ground that there has been no *bonâ fide* user of such trade mark in connection with such goods during the five years immediately preceding the application, unless in either case such non-user is shown to be due to special circumstances in the trade, and not to any intention not to use or to abandon such trade mark in respect of such goods.

Effect of Registration.

38.—Subject to the provisions of this Act—

(1) The person for the time being entered in the register as proprietor of a trade mark shall, subject to any rights appearing from such register to be vested in any other person, have power to assign the same, and to give effectual receipts for any consideration for such assignment :

(2) Any equities in respect of a trade mark may be enforced in like manner as in respect of any other personal property.

39.—Subject to the provisions of section forty-one of this Act and to any limitations and conditions entered upon the register, the registration of a person as proprietor of a trade mark shall, if valid, give to such person the exclusive right to the use of such trade mark upon or in connection with the goods in respect of which it is registered : Provided always that where two or more persons are registered proprietors of the same (or substantially the same) trade mark in respect of the same goods no rights of exclusive user of such trade mark shall (except so far as their respective rights shall have been defined by the Court) be acquired by any one of such persons as against any other by the registration thereof, but each of such persons shall otherwise have the same rights as if he were the sole registered proprietor thereof.

40.—In all legal proceedings relating to a registered trade mark (including applications under section thirty-five of this Act) the fact that a person is registered as proprietor of such trade mark shall be *primâ facie* evidence of the validity of the original registration of such trade mark and of all subsequent assignments and transmissions of the same.

41.—In all legal proceedings relating to a registered trade mark (including applications under section thirty-five of this Act) the original registration of such trade mark shall after the expiration of seven years from the date of such original registration (or seven years from the passing of this Act, whichever shall last happen) be taken to be valid in all respects unless such original registration was obtained by fraud, or unless the trade mark offends against the provisions of section eleven of this Act :

Provided that nothing in this Act shall entitle the proprietor of a registered trade mark to interfere with or restrain the user by any person of a similar trade mark upon or in connection with goods upon or in connection with which such person has, by himself or his predecessors in business, continuously used such trade mark from a date anterior to the user of the first-mentioned trade mark by the proprietor thereof or his predecessors in business, or to object (on such user being proved) to such person being put upon the register for such similar trade mark in respect of such goods under the provisions of section twenty-one of this Act.

42.—No person shall be entitled to institute any proceeding to prevent or to recover damages for the infringement of an unregistered trade mark unless such trade mark was in use before the thirteenth of August one thousand eight hundred and seventy-five, and has been refused registration under this Act. The Registrar may, on request, grant a certificate that such registration has been refused.

43.—In an action for the infringement of a trade mark the Court trying the question of infringement shall admit evidence of the usages of the trade in respect to the get-up of the goods for which the trade mark is registered, and of any trade marks or get-up legitimately used in connection with such goods by other persons.

44.—No registration under this Act shall interfere with any *bonâ fide* use by a person of his own name or place of business or that of any of his predecessors in business, or the use by any person of any *bonâ fide* description of the character or quality of his goods.

45.—Nothing in this Act contained shall be deemed to affect rights of action against any person for passing off goods as those of another person or the remedies in respect thereof.

Legal Proceedings.

46.—In any legal proceedings in which the validity of the registration of a registered trade mark comes into question, and is decided in favour of the proprietor of such trade mark, the Court may certify the same, and if it so certifies then in any subsequent legal proceeding in which such validity comes into question the proprietor of the said trade mark on obtaining a final order or judgment in his favour shall have his full costs, charges, and expenses as between solicitor and client, unless in such subsequent proceeding the Court certifies that he ought not to have the same.

47.—In any legal proceeding in which the relief sought includes alteration or rectification of the register, the Registrar shall have the right to appear and be heard, and shall appear if so directed by the Court. Unless otherwise directed by the Court, the Registrar in lieu of appearing and being heard may submit to the Court a statement in writing signed by him, giving particulars of the proceedings before him in relation to the matter in issue or of the grounds of any decision given by him affecting the same or of the practice of the office in like cases, or of such other matters relevant to the issues, and within his knowledge as such Registrar, as he shall think fit, and such statement shall be deemed to form part of the evidence in the proceeding.

Costs.

48.—In all proceedings before the Court under this Act the costs of the Registrar shall be in the discretion of the Court, but the Registrar shall not be ordered to pay the costs of any other of the parties.

Evidence.

49.—In any proceeding under this Act before the Board of Trade or the Registrar, the evidence shall be given by statutory declaration in the absence of directions to the contrary, but, in any case in which it shall think it right so to do, the tribunal may (with the consent of the parties) take evidence *vivâ voce* in lieu of or in addition to evidence by declaration. Any such statutory declaration may in the case of appeal be used before the Court in lieu of evidence by affidavit, but if so used shall have all the incidents and consequences of evidence by affidavit.

In case any part of the evidence is taken *vivâ voce* the Board of Trade or the Registrar shall in respect of requiring the attendance of witnesses and taking evidence on oath be in the same position in all respects as an Official Referee of the Supreme Court.

50.—Printed or written copies or extracts of or from the register, purporting to be certified by the Registrar and sealed with the seal of the Patent Office, shall be admitted in evidence in all Courts in His Majesty's dominions, and in all proceedings, without further proof or production of the originals.

51.—A certificate purporting to be under the hand of the Registrar as to any entry, matter, or thing, which he is authorised by this Act, or rules made thereunder, to make or do, shall be *primâ facie* evidence of the entry having been made, and of the contents thereof, and of the matter or thing having been done or not done.

52.—(1) All documents purporting to be orders made by the Board of Trade and to be sealed with the seal of the Board, or to be signed by a secretary or assistant secretary of the Board or by any person authorised in that behalf by the President of the Board, shall be received in evidence, and shall be deemed to be such orders without further proof, unless the contrary is shown.

(2) A certificate, signed by the President of the Board of Trade, that any order made or act done is the order or act of the Board, shall be conclusive evidence of the fact so certified.

PART II.

Powers and Duties of Registrar of Trade Marks.

53.—Where any discretionary or other power is given to the Registrar by this Act or rules made thereunder he shall not exercise that power adversely to the applicant for registration or the registered proprietor of the trade mark in question without (if duly required so to do within the prescribed time) giving such applicant or registered proprietor an opportunity of being heard.

54.—Except where expressly given by the provisions of this Act or rules made thereunder there shall be no appeal from a decision of the Registrar otherwise than to the Board of Trade, but the Court, in dealing with any question of the rectification of the register (including all applications under the provisions of section thirty-five of this Act), shall have power to review any decision of the Registrar relating to the entry in question or the correction sought to be made.

55.—Where by this Act any act has to be done by or to any person in connection with a trade mark or proposed trade mark or any procedure relating thereto, such act may under and in accordance with rules made under this Act or in particular cases by special leave of the Board of Trade be done by or to an agent of such party duly authorised in the prescribed manner.

56.—The Registrar may, in any case of doubt or difficulty arising in the administration of any of the provisions of this Act, apply to His Majesty's Attorney-General or Solicitor-General for England for directions in the matter.

57.—The Comptroller General of Patents, Designs, and Trade Marks shall in his yearly report on the execution by or under him of the Patents, Designs, and Trade Marks Act, 1883, and Acts amending the same, include a report respecting the execution by or under him of this Act as though it formed a part of or was included in such Acts.

Powers and Duties of the Board of Trade.

58.—All things required or authorised under this Act to be done by to or before the Board of Trade may be done by to or before the President or a secretary or an assistant secretary of the Board or any person authorised in that behalf by the President of the Board.

59.—Where under this Act an appeal is made to the Board of Trade, the Board of Trade may, if they think fit, refer any such appeal to the Court in lieu of hearing and deciding it themselves, but, unless the Board so refer the appeal, it shall be heard and decided by the Board, and the decision of the Board shall be final.

60.—(1) Subject to the provisions of this Act the Board of Trade may from time to time make such rules, prescribe such forms, and generally do such things as they think expedient—

(*a*) For regulating the practice under this Act :

(*b*) For classifying goods for the purposes of registration of trade marks :

(*c*) For making or requiring duplicates of trade marks and other documents :

(*d*) For securing and regulating the publishing and selling or distributing in such manner as the Board of Trade think fit, of copies of trade marks and other documents :

(*e*) Generally, for regulating the business of the office in relation to trade marks and all things by this Act placed under the direction or control of the Registrar, or of the Board of Trade.

(2) Rules made under this section shall, whilst in force, be of the same effect as if they were contained in this Act.

(3) Before making any rules under this section the Board of Trade shall publish notice of their intention to make the rules and of the place where copies of the draft rules may be obtained in such manner as the Board consider most expedient, so as to enable persons affected to make representations to the Board before the rules are finally settled.

(4) Any rules made in pursuance of this section shall be forthwith advertised twice in the *Trade Marks Journal,* and shall be laid before both Houses of Parliament, if Parliament be in session at the time of making thereof, or, if not, then as soon as practicable after the beginning of the then next session of Parliament.

(5) If either House of Parliament within the next forty days after any rules have been so laid before such House, resolve that such rules or any of them ought to be annulled, the same shall after the date of such resolution be of no effect, without prejudice to the validity of anything done in the meantime under such rules or rule or to the making of any new rules or rule.

Fees.

61.—There shall be paid in respect of applications and registration and other matters under this Act, such fees as may be, with the sanction of the Treasury, prescribed by the Board of Trade.

Special Trade Marks.

62.—Where any association or person undertakes the examination of any goods in respect of origin, material, mode of manufacture, quality, accuracy, or other characteristic, and certifies the result of such examination by mark used upon or in connection with such goods, the Board of Trade may, if they shall judge it to be to the public advantage, permit such association or person to register such mark as a trade mark in respect of such goods, whether or not such association or person be a trading association or trader or possessed of a Goodwill in connection with such examination and certifying. When so registered such trade mark shall be deemed in all respects to be a registered trade mark, and such association or person to be the proprietor thereof, save that such trade mark shall be transmissible or assignable only by permission of the Board of Trade.

Sheffield Marks.

63.—With respect to the master, wardens, searchers, assistants, and commonalty of the Company of Cutlers in Hallamshire, in the county of York (in this Act called the Cutlers' Company), and the marks or devices (in this Act called Sheffield marks) assigned or registered by the master, wardens, searchers, and assistants of that company, the following provisions shall have effect :—

(1) The Cutlers' Company shall continue to keep at Sheffield the register of trade marks (in this Act called the Sheffield Register) kept by them at the date of the commencement of this Act, and, save as otherwise provided by this Act, such register shall for all purposes form part of the register :

(2) The Cutlers' Company shall, on request made in the prescribed manner, enter in the Sheffield Register, in respect of metal goods as defined in this section, all the trade marks which shall have been assigned by the Cutlers' Company and actually used before the first day of January one thousand eight hundred and eighty-four, but which have not been entered in such register before the passing of this Act :

(3) An application for registration of a trade mark used on metal goods shall, if made after the commencement of this Act by a person carrying on business in Hallamshire, or within six miles thereof, be made to the Cutlers' Company :

(4) Every application so made to the Cutlers' Company shall be notified to the Registrar in the prescribed manner, and, unless the Registrar within the prescribed time gives notice to the Cutlers' Company of any objection to the acceptance of

the application, it shall be proceeded with by the Cutlers' Company in the prescribed manner :

(5) If the Registrar gives notice of an objection as aforesaid, the application shall not be proceeded with by the Cutlers' Company, but any person aggrieved may in the prescribed manner appeal to the Court :

(6) Upon the registration of a trade mark in the Sheffield Register the Cutlers' Company shall give notice thereof to the Registrar, who shall thereupon enter the mark in the Register of Trade Marks; and such registration shall bear date as of the day of application to the Cutlers' Company, and have the same effect as if the application had been made to the Registrar on that day :

(7) The provisions of this Act, and of any rules made under this Act with respect to the registration of trade marks, and all matters relating thereto, shall, subject to the provisions of this section (and notwithstanding anything in any Act relating to the Cutlers' Company), apply to the registration of trade marks on metal goods by the Cutlers' Company, and to all matters relating thereto; and this Act and any such rules shall, so far as applicable, be construed accordingly with the substitution of the Cutlers' Company, the office of the Cutlers' Company, and the Sheffield Register, for the Registrar, the Patent Office, and the Register of Trade Marks respectively; and notice of every entry, cancellation, or correction made in the Sheffield Register shall be given to the Registrar by the Cutlers' Company :

(8) When the Registrar receives from any person not carrying on business in Hallamshire or within six miles thereof an application for registration of a trade mark used on metal goods, he shall in the prescribed manner notify the application and proceedings thereon to the Cutlers' Company :

(9) Any person aggrieved by a decision of the Cutlers' Company in respect of anything done or omitted under this Act may, in the prescribed manner, appeal to the Court :

(10) For the purposes of this section the expression "metal goods" means all metals, whether wrought, unwrought, or partly wrought, and all goods composed wholly or partly of any metal :

(11) For the purpose of legal proceedings in relation to trade marks entered in the Sheffield Register a certificate under the hand of the Master of the Cutlers' Company shall have the same effect as the certificate of the Registrar.

Cotton Marks.

64.—(1) The Manchester Branch of the Trade Marks Registry of the Patent Office (hereinafter called "the Manchester Branch") shall be continued according to its present constitution. A chief officer of the Manchester Branch shall be appointed who shall be styled "the Keeper of Cotton Marks," and shall act under the direction of the Registrar. The present keeper of the Manchester Branch shall be the first Keeper of Cotton Marks.

(2) As regards cotton goods which have hitherto constituted classes 23, 24, and 25, under the classification of goods under the Patents, Designs, and Trade Marks Acts, 1883 to 1902, the Register of Trade Marks for all such goods, except such as may be prescribed, shall be called "the Manchester Register," and a duplicate thereof shall be kept at the Manchester Branch.

(3) All applications for registration of trade marks for such cotton goods in the said classes (hereinafter referred to as "cotton marks") shall be made to the Manchester Branch.

(4) Every application so made to the Manchester Branch shall be notified to the Registrar in the prescribed manner together with the report of the Keeper of Cotton Marks thereon, and unless the Registrar, after considering the report and hearing, if so required, the applicant, within the prescribed time gives notice to the Keeper of Cotton Marks of objection to the acceptance of the application, it shall be advertised by the Manchester Branch and shall be proceeded with in the prescribed manner.

(5) If the Registrar gives notice of objection as aforesaid the application shall not be proceeded with, but any person aggrieved may in the prescribed manner appeal to the Court or the Board of Trade, at the option of the applicant.

(6) Upon the registration of a trade mark in the Manchester Register the Keeper of Cotton Marks shall upon notice thereof from the Registrar thereupon enter the mark in the duplicate of the Manchester Register, and such registration shall bear date as of the day of application to the Manchester Branch, and shall have the same effect as if the application had been made to the Registrar on that day.

(7) When any mark is removed from or any cancellation or correction made in the Manchester Register notice thereof shall be given by the Registrar to the Keeper of Cotton Marks, who shall alter the duplicate register accordingly.

(8) For the purpose of all proceedings in relation to trade marks entered in the Manchester Register a certificate under the hand of the Keeper of Cotton Marks shall have the same effect as a certificate of the Registrar.

(9) In every application for registration of a cotton mark, if such mark has been used by the applicant or his predecessors in business prior to the date of application, the length of time of such user shall be stated on the application.

(10) As from the passing of this Act—

(a) In respect of cotton piece goods and cotton yarn no mark consisting of a word or words alone (whether invented or otherwise) shall be registered, and no word or words shall be deemed to be distinctive in respect of such goods :

(b) In respect of cotton piece goods no mark consisting of a line heading alone shall be registered, and no line heading shall be deemed to be distinctive in respect of such goods :

(c) No registration of a cotton mark shall give any exclusive right to the use of any word, letter, numeral, line heading, or any combination thereof.

(11) The right of inspection of the Manchester Register shall extend to and include the right to inspect all applications whatsoever that have been since the passing of the Trade Marks Registration Act, 1875, and hereafter shall have been made to the Manchester Branch in respect of cotton goods in classes 23, 24, and 25, whether registered, refused, lapsed, expired, withdrawn, abandoned, cancelled, or pending.

(12) The Keeper of Cotton Marks shall, on request, and on production of a facsimile of the mark, and on payment of the prescribed fee, issue a certified copy of the application for registration of any cotton mark, setting forth in such certificate the length of time of user (if any) of such mark as stated on the application, and any other particulars he may deem necessary.

(13) As regards any rules or forms affecting cotton marks which are proposed by the Board of Trade to be made, the draft of the same shall be sent to the Keeper of Cotton Marks and also to the Manchester Chamber of Commerce. And the said Keeper, and also the said Chamber, shall, if they or either of them so request, be entitled to be heard by the Board of Trade upon such proposed rules before the same are carried into effect.

(14) The existing practice whereby the keeper of the Manchester Branch consults the Trade and Merchandise Marks Committee appointed by the Manchester Chamber of Commerce upon questions of novelty or difficulty arising on applications to register cotton marks shall be continued by the Keeper of Cotton Marks.

International and Colonial Arrangements.

65.—The provisions of sections one hundred and three and one hundred and four of the Patents, Designs, and Trade Marks Act, 1883 (as amended by the Patents, Designs, and Trade Marks (Amendment) Act, 1885), relating to the registration of trade marks both as enacted in such Acts and as applied by any Order in Council made thereunder, shall be construed as applying to trade marks registrable under this Act.

Offences.

66.—If any person makes or causes to be made a false entry in the register kept under this Act, or a writing falsely purporting to be a copy of an entry in any such register, or produces or tenders or causes to be produced or tendered in evidence any such writing, knowing the entry or writing to be false, he shall be guilty of a misdemeanour.

67.—(1) Any person who represents a trade mark as registered which is not so, shall be liable for every offence on summary conviction to a fine not exceeding five pounds.

(2) A person shall be deemed, for the purposes of this enactment, to represent that a trade mark is registered, if he uses in connection with the trade mark the word " registered," or any words expressing or implying that registration has been obtained for the trade mark.

Royal Arms.

68.—If any person, without the authority of His Majesty, uses in connection with any trade, business, calling, or profession, the Royal

Arms (or arms so closely resembling the same as to be calculated to deceive) in such manner as to be calculated to lead to the belief that he is duly authorised so to use the Royal Arms, or if any person without the authority of his Majesty or of a member of the Royal Family, uses in connection with any trade, business, calling, or profession any device, emblem, or title in such manner as to be calculated to lead to the belief that he is employed by or supplies goods to His Majesty or such member of the Royal Family, he may, at the suit of any person who is authorised to use such arms or such device, emblem, or title, or is authorised by the Lord Chamberlain to take proceedings in that behalf, be restrained by injunction or interdict from continuing so to use the same : Provided that nothing in this section shall be construed as affecting the right, if any, of the proprietor of a trade mark containing any such arms, device, emblem, or title to continue to use such trade mark.

Courts.

69.—The provisions of this Act conferring a special jurisdiction on the Court as defined by this Act shall not, except so far as the jurisdiction extends, affect the jurisdiction of any Court in Scotland or Ireland in any proceedings relating to trade marks ; and with reference to any such proceedings in Scotland the term " the Court " shall mean the Court of Session ; and with reference to any such proceedings in Ireland the term " the Court " shall mean the High Court of Justice in Ireland.

70.—This Act shall extend to the Isle of Man, and—

(1) Nothing in this Act shall effect the jurisdiction of the Courts in the Isle of Man in proceedings for infringement or in any action or proceeding respecting a trade mark competent to those Courts :

(2) The punishment for a misdemeanour under this Act in the Isle of Man shall be imprisonment for any term not exceeding two years, with or without hard labour and with or without a fine not exceeding one hundred pounds, at the discretion of the Court :

(3) Any offence under this Act committed in the Isle of Man which would in England be punishable on summary conviction may be prosecuted, and any fine in respect thereof recovered at the instance of any person aggrieved, in the manner in which offences punishable on summary conviction may for the time being be prosecuted.

71.—The Court of Chancery of the County Palatine of Lancaster shall, with respect to any action or other proceeding in relation to trade marks, the registration whereof is applied for in the Manchester Branch, have the like jurisdiction under this Act as His Majesty's High Court of Justice in England, and the expression "the Court" in this Act shall be construed and have effect accordingly :

Provided that every decision of the Court of Chancery of the County Palatine of Lancaster in pursuance of this section shall be subject to the like appeal as decisions of that Court in other cases.

72.—In Scotland any offence under this Act declared to be punishable on summary conviction may be prosecuted in the Sheriff Court.

Repeal; Savings.

73.—The enactments described in the schedule to this Act are repealed to the extent mentioned in the third column, but this repeal shall not affect any rule, table of fees, or classification of goods made under any enactment so repealed, but every such rule, table of fees, or classification of goods shall continue in force as if made under this Act until superseded by rules, tables of fees, or classification under this Act.

74.—The provisions of sections eighty-two to eighty-four of the Patents, Designs, and Trade Marks Act, 1883, as amended by any subsequent enactment, shall continue to apply with respect to the administration at the Patent Office of the law relating to the registration of trade marks, and shall accordingly be construed as if this Act formed part of that Act.

SCHEDULE.
Enactments Repealed.

Session and Chapter	Short Title	Extent of Repeal
46 & 47 Vict. c. 57	The Patents, Designs, and Trade Marks Act, 1883	Sections sixty-two to eighty-one, and, so far as they respectively relate to trade marks, sections eighty-five to ninety-nine, one hundred and one, one hundred and two, one hundred and five, one hundred and eight, and one hundred and eleven to one hundred and seventeen.
51 & 52 Vict. c. 50	The Patents, Designs, and Trade Marks Act, 1888	Sections eight to twenty, and, so far as they respectively relate to trade marks, sections twenty-one to twenty-six.

THE TRADE MARKS ACT, 1919.

(9 & 10 Geo. 5, c. 79.)

An Act to amend the Trade Marks Act, 1905.

[23rd December 1919.]

BE it enacted by the King's most Excellent Majesty, by and with the advice and consent of the Lords Spiritual and Temporal, and Commons, in this present Parliament assembled, and by the authority of the same, as follows :—

PART I.

REGISTRATION OF CERTAIN TRADE MARKS NOT REGISTRABLE UNDER PRINCIPAL ACT.

Division of Register of Trade Marks into Two Parts.

1.—(1) The register of trade marks (including the Manchester Register) kept under the Trade Marks Act, 1905 (hereinafter referred to as the principal Act), shall be divided into two parts to be called respectively Part A. and Part B.

(2) Part A. of the register shall comprise all trade marks entered in the register of trade marks at the commencement of this Act, and all trade marks which after the commencement of this Act may be registered under the provisions of the principal Act.

(3) Part B. shall comprise all trade marks registered under this Part of this Act, and all trade marks entered on or removed thereto under this Act.

Registration of Trade Marks in Part B.

2.—(1) Where any mark has for not less than two years been bonâ fide used in the United Kingdom upon or in connection with any goods (whether for sale in the United Kingdom or exportation abroad), for the purpose of indicating that they are the goods of the proprietor of the mark by virtue of manufacture, selection, certification, dealing with or offering for sale, the person claiming to be the proprietor of the mark may apply in writing to the registrar in the prescribed manner to have the mark entered as his registered trade mark in Part B. of the register in respect of such goods.

(2) The registrar shall consider every such application for registration of a trade mark in Part B. of the register, and if it appears to him, after such search, if any, as he may deem necessary, that the application is inconsistent with the provisions of section eleven or section nineteen of the principal Act, or if he is not satisfied that

the mark has been so used as aforesaid, or that it is capable of distinguishing the goods of the applicant, he may refuse the application, or may accept it subject to conditions, amendments or modifications as to the goods or classes of goods in respect of which the mark is to be registered, or to such limitations, if any, as to mode or place of user or otherwise as he may think right to impose, and in any other case he shall accept the application.

(3) Every such application shall be accompanied by a statutory declaration verifying the user, including the date of first user, and such date shall be entered on the register.

(4) Any such refusal or conditional acceptance shall be subject to appeal to the court, and, if the ground for refusal is insufficiency of evidence as to user, such refusal shall be without prejudice to any application for registration of the trade mark under the provisions of the principal Act.

(5) Every such application shall, if accepted, be advertised in accordance with the provisions of the principal Act.

(6) A mark may be registered in Part B. notwithstanding any registration in Part A. by the same proprietor of the same mark or any part or parts thereof.

Application of certain Provisions of Principal Act to Part B. Trade Marks.

3. The provisions of the principal Act, as amended by this Act, with the exception of those set out in the First Schedule to this Act, shall, subject to the provisions of this Part of this Act, apply in respect of trade marks to which this Part of this Act applies as if they were herein re-enacted and in terms made applicable to this Part of this Act.

Effect of Registration in Part B.

4. The registration of a person as the proprietor of a trade mark in Part B. of the register shall be primâ facie evidence that that person has the exclusive right to the use of that trade mark, but, in any action for infringement of a trade mark entered in Part B. of the register, no injunction, interdict or other relief shall be granted to the owner of the trade mark in respect of such registration, if the defendant establishes to the satisfaction of the court that the user of which the plaintiff complains is not calculated to deceive or to lead to the belief that the goods the subject of such user were goods manufactured, selected, certified, dealt with or offered for sale by the proprietor of the trade mark.

Power to Treat Applications for Registration in Part A. as
Applications for Registration in Part B.

5. If any person applies for the registration of a trade mark under
the principal Act in Part A. of the register, the registrar may, if the
applicant is willing, instead of refusing the application, treat it
as an application for registration in Part B. of the register under
this Part of this Act and deal with the application accordingly.

PART II.

PROVISIONS FOR THE PREVENTION OF ABUSES OF TRADE MARKS.

Removal from Register of Word Trade Marks Used as Names of
Articles.

6.—(1) Where in the case of an article or substance manufactured
under any patent in force at or granted after the passing of this Act,
a word trade mark registered under the principal Act or Part I. of
this Act is the name or only practicable name of the article or substance so manufactured, all rights to the exclusive use of such trade
mark, whether under the common law or by registration (and notwithstanding the provisions of section forty-one of the principal Act),
shall cease upon the expiration or determination of the patent, and
thereafter such word shall not be deemed a distinctive mark, and may
be removed by the court from the register on the application of any
person aggrieved.

(2) No word which is the only practicable name or description of
any single chemical element or single chemical compound, as distinguished from a mixture, shall be registered as a trade mark, and any
such word now or hereafter on the register may, notwithstanding
section forty-one of the principal Act, be removed by the court from
the register on the application of any person aggrieved :

Provided that—

(*a*) the provisions of this subsection shall not apply where the
    mark is used to denote only the proprietor's brand or make
    of such substance, as distinguished from the substance as
    made by others, and in association with a suitable and prac-
    ticable name open to the public use ; and

(*b*) in the case of marks registered before the passing of this Act,
    no application under this section for the removal of the mark
    from the register shall be entertained until after the expira-
    tion of four years from the passing of this Act.

(3) The power to remove a trade mark from the register conferred
by this section shall be in addition to and not in derogation of any

other powers of the court in respect of the removal of trade marks from the register.

(4) The provisions contained in Part III. of this Act authorising applications for the rectification of the register to be made in the first instance to the registrar instead of to the court shall apply to applications under this section.

PART III.
GENERAL AMENDMENTS OF PRINCIPAL ACT.

Amendment of the Law as to Registrable Trade Marks.

7. In paragraph (5) of section nine of the principal Act (which defines the particulars which registrable trade marks must contain or consist of) for the words "except by order of the Board of Trade or the court be deemed a distinctive mark," there shall be substituted the words "be registrable under the provisions of this paragraph, except upon evidence of its distinctiveness."

Appeals.

8.—(1) All appeals from the decisions of the registrar under section fourteen of the principal Act shall be made to the court, and an appeal shall not lie from any such decision to the Board of Trade, and accordingly that section shall have effect, subject to the modifications set forth in the Second Schedule to this Act :

Provided that nothing in this subsection shall affect any appeal which may be pending at the commencement of this Act.

(2) In any appeal from the decision of the registrar to the court under the principal Act or this Act the court shall have and exercise the same discretionary powers as under the principal Act or this Act are conferred upon the registrar.

Rectification of Register.

9.—(1) Any application for the rectification of the register or the removal of any trade mark from the register in respect of any goods which, under section thirty-five or section thirty-seven of the principal Act or under Part II. of this Act, is to be made to the court, may, at the option of the applicant, be made in the first instance to the registrar :

Provided that no such application shall be made otherwise than to the court where an action concerning the trade mark in question is pending.

(2) The registrar may, at any stage of the proceedings, refer any such application to the court or he may, after hearing the parties,

determine the question between them, subject to appeal to the court.

(3) In any proceedings for the rectification of the register under this Act or under section thirty-five of the principal Act as amended by this section the court or the registrar shall, in addition to the powers conferred by that section as so amended, have power to direct a trade mark entered in Part A. of the register to be removed to Part B. of the register.

Costs.

10. In all proceedings before the registrar under the principal Act or this Act the registrar shall have power to award to any party such costs as he may consider reasonable, and to direct how and by what parties they are to be paid, and any such order may be made a rule of court.

11. For section thirty-three of the principal Act. the following section shall be substituted :—

Registration of Assignments.

" 33.—(1) Where a person becomes entitled by assignment, transmission, or other operation of law to a registered trade mark, he shall make application to the registrar to register his title, and the registrar shall, on receipt of such application and on proof of title to his satisfaction, register him as the proprietor of the trade mark, and shall cause an entry to be made in the prescribed manner on the register of the assignment, transmission or other instrument affecting the title. Any decision of the registrar under this section shall be subject to appeal to the court.

" (2) Except in cases of appeals under this section and applications made under section thirty-five of this Act, a document or instrument in respect of which no entry has been made in the register in accordance with the provisions of subsection (1) aforesaid shall not be admitted in evidence in any court in proof of the title to a trade mark unless the court otherwise directs."

Minor Amendments of Principal Act.

12. The amendments specified in the second column of the Second Schedule to this Act, which relate to minor details, shall be made in the provisions of the principal Act specified in the first column of that schedule.

Short Title, Construction and Commencement.

13.—(1) This Act may be cited as the Trade Marks Act, 1919, and the Trade Marks Acts, 1905 and 1914, and so much of the Patents and Designs Acts, 1907 to 1919, as relates to trade marks, and this Act may be cited together as the Trade Marks Acts, 1905 to 1919.

(2) This Act shall be construed as one with the principal Act and shall come into operation on the first day of April nineteen hundred and twenty.

SCHEDULES.

FIRST SCHEDULE.

Provisions of Principal Act not applied.

No. of Section	Subject-matter
1	Short title.
2	Commencement of Act.
6	Incorporation of existing register.
9	Registrable trade marks.
12	Application for registration.
14 (9)	Modification of trade mark on appeals.
15	Disclaimers.
24	Associated trade marks.
25	Combined trade marks.
27	Assignment and user of associated trade mark
31	Status of unrenewed trade marks.
36	Trade marks registered under previous Acts.
39 (except proviso) ..	Rights of proprietor of trade mark.
41 down to the words "against the pro-"visions of section "eleven of this "Act."	Registration to be conclusive after seven years
42	Unregistered trade mark.
62	Standardization, &c., trade marks.
73	Repeal and saving for rules, &c.

SECOND SCHEDULE.

Minor Amendments of Principal Act.

Section Amended	Nature of Amendment
Section 12	At the end of subsection (2) there shall be inserted the following words " or to such limitations, if any, as to mode or "place of user or otherwise as he may think right to im-"pose."
	In subsection (4), after the words " modifications, if any, shall be inserted the words " or to what limitations, if any, " as to mode or place of user or otherwise."
Section 13 ..	After the word "conditions" in both places where it occurs, there shall be inserted the words " and limitations."
	At the end of the section there shall be inserted the words " Provided that an application under the provisions of sub-" section (5) of section nine of this Act may be advertised by "the Registrar on receipt of such application and before "acceptance."
Section 14.. ..	In subsection (4), after the word " conditions " there shall be inserted the following words " or what limitations as to " mode or place of user or otherwise."
	In subsection (5) the words " or with the consent of the " parties to the Board of Trade " shall be repealed.
	In subsection (6) the words "the Board of Trade or" and "as the case may be " shall be repealed; and after the words "conditions, if any," there shall be inserted the words " or what limitations, if any, as to mode or place of "user or otherwise."
	Subsection (10) shall be repealed.

Section Amended	Nature of Amendment
Section 16..	After the words " the registrar shall " there shall be inserted the words " unless the mark has been accepted in error or."
Section 21..	After the word "court " there shall be inserted the words " or registrar " in each case. Delete the words " as it may think it right to impose " and insert " as the court or the registrar, as the case may be, " may think it right to impose."
Section 22..	At the end of the section there shall be added the following words "and the assignment of such right to use the same " shall constitute the assignee a proprietor of a separate " trade mark for the purpose of section twenty-one of this " Act, subject to such conditions and limitations as may be " imposed under that section."
Section 23..	After the words "modifications, if any," there shall be inserted the words " and to such limitations, if any, as to mode or " place of user."
Section 24..	After the words "registration of a trade mark " there shall be inserted the words " identical with or."
Section 34..	After the word "terms" there shall be inserted the words "and subject to such limitations as to mode or place of " user."
Section 41..	In the proviso, after the words "anterior to the user " there shall be inserted the words " or registration, whichever is " the earlier."
Section 43..	For section forty-three the following section shall be substituted : " In any action or proceeding relating to a trade " mark or trade name the tribunal shall admit evidence of " the usages of the trade concerned and of any relevant " trade mark or trade name or get up legitimately used by " other persons."
Section 62..	For the words "Where any association or person undertakes " the examination of any goods in respect of origin, material, " mode of manufacture, quality, accuracy or other charac- " teristic, and certifies the result of such examination by " mark used upon or in connection with such goods, the " Board of Trade may, if they shall judge it to be to the " public advantage, permit such association or person to " register such mark as a trade mark in respect of such " goods whether or not such association or person be a " trading association or trader or possessed of a goodwill in " connection with such examination and certifying," there shall be substituted the words "Where any association or " person undertakes to certify the origin, material, mode of " manufacture, quality, accuracy or other characteristic of " any goods by mark used upon or in connection with such " goods, the Board of Trade, if and so long as they are satis- " fied that such association or person is competent to certify " as aforesaid, may, if they shall judge it to be to the public " advantage, permit such association or person to register " such mark as a trade mark in respect of such goods, " whether or not such association or person be a trading " association or trader or possessed of a goodwill in con- " nection with such certifying."
Section 64..	Subsection (10 (a)) shall be repealed. In subsection (10 (c)) the word "word " shall be omitted.

APPENDIX B.

COMMON FORM CLAUSES RELATING TO GOODWILL.

Contract for the Sale of a Business to a Company (Palmer's Company Precedents, Vol. I., p. 283).—" The vendor shall sell, and "the company shall purchase : First, the Goodwill of the said busi-"ness [with the exclusive right to use the name of M. & Co. as part "of the name of the company, and represent the company as carry-"ing on such business in continuation of the vendor's firm, and in "succession thereto, and the right to use the words ' late M. & Co.,' "or any other words indicating that the business is carried on in "continuation of or succession to the said firm], and all trade marks "connected therewith."

It is safer to include the words in brackets.

Contract for the Sale of a Business to a Private Purchaser (Key and Elphinstone, Vol. I., p. 372).—" The vendors agree to sell, and the " purchaser agrees to purchase, for the sum of £—— the Goodwill of "the business known as ' ————,' being one of the businesses "carried on by the vendors in co-partnership at ————, together "with the right to carry on such business under the name or style "of ————, and also the exclusive right to use the brand or trade "mark ———— on (certain articles), reserving to the vendors the "right to use the said brand or trade mark on (certain other articles). "And the vendors will not at any time solicit any of the customers of "the said late firm."

If the vendors are giving up business altogether the last clause will be omitted, and the vendors will agree not to carry on a competing business. (See next form.)

Covenant by Vendor not to Compete (Encyclopædia of Forms and Precedents, Vol. VI., p. 169).—The vendor hereby covenants with the purchaser that the vendor will not within —— years from the date hereof either solely or jointly with, or as manager or agent for, any person or corporation directly or indirectly carry on, or be engaged or interested in, the business of ————, nor permit his name to be used in connection with any such business within —— miles of ————.

Contract for Sale by Liquidator of a Company of the Business as a Going Concern (Key and Elphinstone, Vol. I., p. 374).—"The ven-"dors shall sell, and the purchasers shall purchase, for the sum of "£——, and upon the terms and subject as hereinafter mentioned.

"(3) All patent rights and trade marks belonging to the vendors "in connection with their said business, and the Goodwill of the "said business as a going concern, with the right to use the name "of the vendors in connection therewith; and (4) the business books "of the vendors at their place of business ————.

"Upon the completion of the purchase a circular in a form to be "approved by the vendors' solicitors shall be sent by the vendors to "all their customers and agents, announcing the transfer of the said "business and Goodwill to the purchasers."

CLAUSES IN PARTNERSHIP ARTICLES (Key and Elphinstone, Vol. XI., p. 343) :—

Allowance for Goodwill.—"On the death or retirement of any "partner an allowance [or ' no allowance '] shall be made to him or "his representatives in respect of the value of the Goodwill of the "said business."

Valuation of Goodwill.—"In any case in which it may become "necessary to value the Goodwill of the said business, the same shall, "unless otherwise agreed, be taken to be equivalent in value to *three* "times the average net yearly profits of the said business during the "*three* preceding years, or from the commencement of the partner- "ship if less than that time."

Goodwill not to be Sold on Dissolution (Encyclopædia of Forms and Precedents, Vol. VI., p. 152-3).—"On the dissolution of the "partnership the Goodwill of the business shall not be sold, but each

" partner shall be at liberty to commence and carry on a similar
" business in his own or any other name not being identical with
" the name of the firm, and to send circulars to the customers of the
" firm announcing the facts of such dissolution and commencement of
" business."

Goodwill to be Sold on Dissolution.—" On the dissolution of the
" partnership, if the said business is sold as a going concern, the
" Goodwill shall be treated as a partnership asset, and no partner
" (unless he shall be the purchaser of such business) shall for —— years
" from the completion of such sale directly or indirectly carry on or
" be concerned or interested in the business of a ———— as principal,
" agent, manager, traveller, or servant within —— miles of ——."

INDEX OF CASES.

	PAGE
Abstainers & General Insurance Co., *In re*	73
American Leather Cloth Co., Lim., Leather Cloth Co., Lim. *v.*	23, 32, 35
Angus, Inland Revenue *v.*	50
Arundel *v.* Bell	47, 48
Austen *v.* Boys	47, 48
Australian Wines, Lim., *In re*	22
Badman, Pinto *v.*	5, 23
Banham, Reddaway *v.*	35, 38, 39
Banks *v.* Gibson	61
Barrow *v.* Barrow	67, 72
Barrow Hæmatite Steel Co., *In re*	72
Barrows, Hall *v.*	24, 26, 65
Bell, Arundel *v.*	47, 48
Birmingham Vinegar Co., Powell *v.*	14
Booth *v.* Curtis	51
Boys, Austen *v.*	47, 48
British & American Shoe Co., Lim., H. E. Randall, Lim. *v.*	19
Burberrys *v.* Cording	39
Burchell *v.* Wilde	60, 62, 69
Burgess *v.* Burgess	38
Cadburys Brothers' Application, *In re*	32
Cash *v.* Cash	13
Cellular Clothing Co. *v.* Manton	36
Churton *v.* Douglas	44, 61
Clements, Shipwright *v.*	7, 53
Collingridge, Cook *v.*	65
Commissioners of Inland Revenue *v.* Muller, Lim.	2, 46, 50, 51
Condy *v.* Mitchell	37
Cook *v.* Collingridge	65
Cooper & Co., Ginesi *v.*	45
Crawford & Sons' Application, *In re*	32
Croft *v.* Day	12

PAGE

Crosfield & Sons' Application, *In re* .. 30
Crutwell *v.* Lye 43, 44, 46
Curl Brothers, Lim. *v.* Webster 57
Currie, Wotherspoon *v.* 36
Curtis, Booty *v.* 51

Daimler Co.'s Application, *In re* .. 32
David & Matthews, *In re* 43, 53, 64, 66
Dawson, Labouchere *v.* 54, 58
Day, Croft *v.*.. 12
Dennis, Edwards *v.* 27
Douglas, Churton *v.* 44, 61
Dowling, Hunter *v.* 51, 68
Downs, England *v.* 44

Edwards *v.* Dennis 27
England *v.* Downs 44

Fearis, Hill *v.* 2, 3, 48, 60, 64, 65
Fine Cotton Spinners' Association,Lim. *v.*Harwood,Cash & Co. 16, 17

Gibson, Banks *v.* 61
Ginesi, *v.* Cooper & Co. 45
Gladstone, Steuart *v.* 47, 67, 71, 72
Grahame, Ransome *v.* 21
Green & Son (Northampton), Lim. *v.* Morris 59

Hall *v.* Barrows 24, 26, 65
Hanbury, Liebig's Extract of Meat Co. *v.* 37
Hill *v.* Fearis 2, 3, 48, 60, 64, 65
Hill, Thorniloe *v.* 4, 33
Horlick's Malted Milk Co. *v.* Summerskill 36
Hunt, Trego *v.* .. 42, 45, 48, 49, 54, 57, 58, 59, 65, 67
Hunter *v.* Dowling 51, 68

Imperial Tobacco's Co.'s Trade Mark, *In re* .. 34
Inland Revenue *v.* Angus 50

Jamieson *v.* Jamieson 14
Jarman, Townsend *v.* 57, 69
Jenkins, Wade *v.* 67, 72
Jennings *v.* Jennings 53, 58

PAGE

Kingston, Miller & Co. v. Thos. Kingston & Co., Lim.   .. 16, 49

Labouchere v. Dawson 54, 58
Leather Cloth Co. v. The American Leather Cloth Co.   23, 32, 35
Levy v. Walker 12, 61, 62
Liebig's Extract of Meat Co. v. Hanbury   37
Lye, Crutwell v. 43, 44, 46

Major Bros. v. Franklin & Sons   22
Manton, Cellular Clothing Co. v.   36
Massam v. Thorley's Cattle Food Co.   23
Maxim Nordenfeldt, Nordenfeldt v.   57
May v. Thomson   48
Merchant Banking Co. v. Merchants' Joint Stock Bank ..   11
Mitchell, Condy v.   37
Mottram, Walker v. 50, 57, 58, 59
Muller, Lim., Commissioners of Inland Revenue v.   2, 46, 50, 51
Murrati's Application, In re   32

Nelson, Smith v. 68, 71
Nordenfeldt v. Maxim Nordenfeldt ..   57

Ord, Sidney & Co.'s Trade Mark, In re

                                                    8

Pearks, Gunston & Tee, Lim. v. Thompson, Talmey & Co.   18
Philippart's Trade Mark, In re   29
Pinto v. Badman 5, 23
Powell v. Birmingham Vinegar Co.   14
Powell's Trade Mark, In re   22

Quiddington, Robertson v.   51, 54

Randall (H. E.), Lim. v. The British & American Shoe Co. ..   19
Ransome v. Grahame   21
Reddaway v. Banham 35, 38, 39
Registrar of Trade Marks v. Du Cros, Lim.   25
Robertson v. Quiddington 51, 54
Rowland, Scott v.   ·   60
Russell, Ex parte   70

PAGE

Scott *v.* Rowland 60
Shipwright *v.* Clements 7, 53
Shove, Thynne *v.* 60, 62
Smith *v.* Nelson 68, 71
Spalding Bros. *v.* A. W. Gamage, Lim. .. 24, 37
Steuart *v.* Gladstone 47, 67, 71, 72

Teofani, Lim. *v.* A. Teofani 31
The American Leather Cloth Co., Leather Cloth Co. *v.* .. 23, 32, 35
The British & American Shoe Co., Randall (H. E.), Lim. *v.* .. 19
Thompson, Talmey & Co., Pearks, Gunston & Tee, Lim. *v.* .. 18
Thomson, May *v.* 48
Thorley's Cattle Food Co., Massam *v.* 23
Thorniloe *v.* Hill 4, 33
Thynne *v.* Shove 60, 62
Townsend *v.* Jarman 57, 69
Trego *v.* Hunt .. 42, 45, 48, 49, 54, 57, 58, 59, 65, 67

Wade *v.* Jenkins 67, 72
Walker, Levy *v.* .. 12, 61, 62
Walker *v.* Mottram .. 50, 57, 58, 59
Webster, Curl Brothers, Lim. *v.* .. 57
Wilde, Burchell *v.* .. 60, 62, 69
William's Application, *In re* .. 29
Williams, Wilson *v.* 65
Wilson *v.* Williams 65
Wotherspoon *v.* Currie 36

INDEX.

	PAGE
Admission of additional partner, Treatment of Goodwill on ..	116
Agreement not to ompete	54
Amalgamation of business, Treatment of Goodwill on ..	107
,, companies, Treatment of Goodwill on ..	141
Annual Accounts, Fluctuations of Goodwill disregarded in ..	90
,, Goodwill not included in ..	67, 68, 71, 91
,, When Goodwill included in ..	.. 93, 94
Apportionment of partnership insurance premiums between partners	.. 76, 77
Assignee of Goodwill, Rights of	54
Assignment of Goodwill by trustee	.. 57, 58
,, ,, Right to use trade name on ..	54
,, trade name, No separate	4
Assignor of Goodwill, Competition by	54
Averages, No reliability of, as basis for valuation of Goodwill ..	90
Bankruptcy Act, Section 47	70
Branch business, Valuation of Goodwill	78
Business, Goodwill inseparable from	43
,, more than tangible assets	1
,, Transfer of, passes Goodwill	53
Capital, Goodwill on petition for reduction of	73
,, New issues of	
Carrier's business, Goodwill of	43
Cases, Trade-mark defined by	21
Chance trade, Goodwill of	83
Common form clauses relating to Goodwill	173
,, law trade-mark	24, 25, 35
,, manufacture, No trade-mark for	37
Companies' Accounts, Goodwill in	131
,, Act, 1908, Section 63	18
,, ,, ,, ,, 81	53
,, Identical names not allowed	10
,, Treatment of Goodwill on amalgamation of ..	141
Company Accounts, How cost of Goodwill treated in ..	97
,, Goodwill in accounts of	72
,, under Act of 1862, Right of, to use a fancy name ..	10
Compensation cases, Goodwill in	86
Compete, Agreement not to	54
Competition by assignor of Goodwill	54
,, Effect of, on value of Goodwill	75
Cost of Goodwill, How treated in accounts of company ..	98
,, ,, ,, partnership ..	97
,, management, Value of Goodwill affected by	80

PAGE

Creation of Goodwill 94

Death of partner, Treatment of Goodwill on 123

Deceased partner, Payment out of, by partnership insurance .. 76

Dissolution of partnership, Sale of Goodwill on 64

,, ,, Use of name on 68

Fancy name attached to a particular business 10

,, Right of limited company to use 10

,, ,, to use 10

Final Partnership Accounts, Goodwill in 67

Fluctuations in value of Goodwill 88

,, of Goodwill disregarded in annual accounts .. 90

Foreign or colonial trade, Sale of trade-mark for 62

Fraud upon public by trade-mark 5

Goodwill, Absence of valuation of 79

,, and partnership insurance 76

,, ,, secret reserves 105

,, Assignment of, by trustee 57, 59

,, Circumstances under which a valuation is required .. 75

,, Competition by assignor of 54

,, Creation of 94

,, defined in various cases 43

,, Different elements in 44

,, Disappearance of 8

,, Effect of competition on value of 75

,, Fluctuations in value of 88

,, in accounts of company 72, 124

,, Inclusion of, in Partnership Accounts 67

,, in compensation cases 86

,, ,, Partnership Accounts 67, 107

,, ,, reduction petitions 73

,, inseparable from the business 43, 50

,, is property 50

,, Local situation of 50

,, may be real or personal property 51, 54

,, ,, pass by will 53

,, No reliability of averages as basis for valuation of .. 90

,, not an available asset for debts 70

,, ,, included in annual accounts 66, 67, 70, 71

,, of branch business, Valuation of 78

,, ,, chance trade 83

,, ,, carrier's business 43

,, ,, different classes of business, Valuation of .. 84

	PAGE
Goodwill of partnership is personal property ..	51
,, ,, professional practice	47
,, ,, stone merchant's business	45
,, ,, stuff merchant's business	44
,, Partner's right to a sale of	64
,, passes by transfer of business	52
,, Preliminary definition of..	1
,, Rights of assignee of	44
,, ,, purchaser of	
,, Sale of ,.	52
,, *The Times* on	105
,, to be mentioned in prospectus	53
,, Treatment of, on admission of additional partner	116
,, ,, amalgamation of businesses	107
,, ,, death of partner ..	123
,, ,, retirement of partner ..	126
,, Valuation of	74
,, Value of, affected by cost of management	80
,, ,, interest on capital	80
,, ,, tenure of business premises ..	81
,, when included in Annual Accounts	93
,, ,, paid for in shares of company	87
,, Writing down value of 91, 93, 95, 112, 119, 122, 125, 130, 132, 142	
Identical names not allowed for companies	10
Insurance, partnership, and Goodwill	76
,, ,, Apportionment of premiums between partners	77
,, . ,, Payment out of deceased partner by ..	77
Interest on capital, Value of Goodwill affected by	80
Partner, Treatment of Goodwill on death of	123
,, ,, retirement of	126
Partner's right to a sale of Goodwill	64
,, set up rival business	65
Partnership Accounts, Goodwill in 67, 107	
,, ,, How cost of Goodwill treated in ..	97
,, ,, Inclusion of Goodwill in	67
,, Goodwill of, is common property	64
,, ,, personal property	51
,, insurance and Goodwill	76
,, ,, Apportionment of premiums between partners	77

PAGE

Partnership Accounts, Payment out of deceased partner by   77

  ,,   name, Use after dissolution   68

  ,,   Sale of Goodwill on dissolution of   64

  ,,   Use of name on dissolution of   68

Payment out of deceased partner by partnership insurance   77

Pro rata issues of Capital

Professional practice, Goodwill of   47

Property in trade-mark   23

Prospectus, Goodwill to be mentioned in   53

Purchaser of Goodwill, Rights of ..,   74

Passing off Goods   34-9

Real name, How far Courts will restrain from using   11, 16, 17

Reduction petitions, Goodwill in   73

Retirement of partner, Treatment of Goodwill on   126

Right in gross explained   4

  ,,   of company under Act of 1862 to use a fancy name   10

Rights of assignee of Goodwill   54

  ,,   purchaser of Goodwill   74

Rival business, Partner's right to set up   65

Sale of Goodwill   52

Secret reserves and Goodwill   105

Stone merchant's business, Goodwill of   55

Stuff merchant's business, Goodwill of   54

Tangible assets, Business more than   1

Tenure of business premises, Value of Goodwill affected by   81

Text of Trade Marks Act, 1905   143

      ,,   1919   166

The Times on Goodwill   105

Trade-mark, Common law   24, 25, 35

  ,,   defined by cases   21

  ,,   ,,   statute   26

  ,,   Fraud upon public by   5

  ,,   limited by actual user   22

  ,,   Names as   29-32, 34-39, 41-42

  ,,   None for common manufacture   37

  ,,   No separate assignment of   4

  ,,   Property in   23

  ,,   Register of   25

  ,,   regulated by statute ..   26

  ,,   Sale for foreign or colonial trade   62

Trade Marks Act, 1875 ..   24, 25, 39

  ,,   ,,   ,,   1905, Section 3   25-34, 41

	PAGE
Trade Marks Act, 1905, Section 8	.. 26, 27
,, ,, ,, ,, ,, 9	.. 28, 30, 34, 41
,, ,, ,, ,, ,, 11	32, 34, 39
,, ,, ,, ,, ,, 12-18	.. 33
,, ,, ,, ,, ,, 19	.. 40
,, ,, ,, ,, ,, 22	.. 9, 52
,, ,, ,, ,, ,, 28-31	.. 33
,, ,, ,, ,, ,, 35	.. 9
,, ,, ,, ,, ,, 40	.. 33
,, ,, ,, ,, ,, 41	34, 41, 42
,, ,, ,, ,, ,, 45	.. 34
,, ,, ,, ,, Text of ..	.. 143
,, name, No separate assignment of	.. 4
,, ,, not property	.. 14
,, ,, Right to a ..	.. 11
,, ,, ,, protection of	.. 10
,, ,, ,, use, on assignment of Goodwill	.. 54
Trade Marks Act, 1919, Part I ..	.. 25
,, ,, ,, ,, ,, II ..	.. 26, 41
,, ,, ,, ,, ,, III ..	26
,, ,, ,, ,, Section 2	.. 39
,, ,, ,, ,, Text of ..	.. 166
Transfer of business, Goodwill passes by	.. 52
Treatment of Goodwill on amalgamation of companies	.. 141
Trustee, Assignment of Goodwill by	.. 58, 59
Valuation, Circumstances under which one is required	.. 75
,, of Goodwill,	.. 74
,, ,, Absence of	.. 79
,, ,, No reliability of averages as basis for	90
Valuation of Goodwill of branch business ..	.. 78
,, ,, different classes of business	.. 84
Value of Goodwill affected by cost of management ..	.. 80
,, ,, interest on capital	.. 80
,, ,, tenure of business premises	.. 81
,, Effect of competition on	.. 75
,, Fluctuations in	.. 88
,, Writing down .. 91, 93, 95, 112, 119, 122, 125, 130, 132, 142	
" Watering " of Capital ..	.. 135
Will, Goodwill may pass by	.. 53
Writing down value of Goodwill 91, 93, 95, 112, 119, 122, 125, 130, 132, 142